EVANGELISM

THE EERDMANS Michael Green COLLECTION

Adventure of Faith:
Reflections on Fifty Years of Christian Service

Baptism:
Its Purpose, Practice, and Power

The Empty Cross of Jesus:
Seeing the Cross in the Light of the Resurrection

Evangelism:
Learning from the Past

Evangelism in the Early Church:
Lessons from the Early Christians for the Church Today

Evangelism through the Local Church:
A Comprehensive Guide to All Aspects of Evangelism

I Believe in Satan's Downfall:
The Reality of Evil and the Victory of Christ

I Believe in the Holy Spirit:
God's Movement in the Church

The Meaning of Salvation:
Redemption and Hope for Today

Thirty Years That Changed the World:
The Book of Acts for Today

EVANGELISM

Learning from the Past

Michael Green

William B. Eerdmans Publishing Company
Grand Rapids, Michigan

Wm. B. Eerdmans Publishing Co.
4035 Park East Court SE, Grand Rapids, Michigan 49546
www.eerdmans.com

Published 2023
Printed in the United States of America

29 28 27 26 25 24 23   1 2 3 4 5 6 7

ISBN 978-0-8028-8343-8

Library of Congress Cataloging-in-Publication Data

A catalog record for this book is available from the Library of
Congress.

Contents

Foreword

by David M. Gustafson

Michael Green (1930–2019) is among the most respected evangelists and scholars of evangelism in the world. He is known widely for his book *Evangelism in the Early Church*, a text that surveys the practice of evangelism in the first three centuries of Christianity. I always wished he would write a history of evangelism that spanned the church's entire history. He has done just that with *Evangelism: Learning from the Past*. In this volume, Michael Green examines evangelism from Jesus and the apostles to the present day. He covers the well-known evangelists and introduces us to lesser-known ones.

I am grateful to the Green family for having Michael's book, which he completed before his death, published posthumously. Michael Green was welcomed into glory in 2019. Despite our loss, we have the joy of reading these final words on the subject of evangelism.

Michael Green's work in the field spanned some sixty years—from his ministry as a parish priest to a seminary professor, from Britain to America, back and forth. He wrote more than fifty books on subjects that range from evangelism, to the Holy Spirit, and to apologetics. I have benefited from his books, such as *Evangelism through the Local Church* (1990). His view of evangelism has been wide as he covered the scope of evangelistic contexts and methods. I have already mentioned his notable work, *Evangelism in the Early Church* (1970). I confess that I drew heavily upon it in my own studies and writing. I say this as a credit to Michael's scholarship.

Now in this present book, *Evangelism: Learning from the Past*, we are reminded of Michael's passion to equip Christians for evangelism. His selection of evangelists from history shows his grasp of those who are inspirational and practical for us today. Michael has always been known for his rare blend of being a scholar and a practitioner, of being a pastor-teacher and an evangelist. In my years of academia, I have noticed how evangelists often become impatient with rigorous research and writing, preferring to spend their time out and about meeting people, ministering in different contexts, and sharing the good news of Jesus. Michael Green, however, did not avoid the rigor of a scholar. He was an evangelist *and* a scholar of evangelism, and we have benefited.

A Christian's perception of evangelism is shaped by the models that he or she has seen. For the past two thousand years, Christians have practiced various means and methods to communicate the gospel. In this book, Michael expands our perceptions of the evangelistic task. He helps us to appreciate and learn from evangelists of earlier generations. He alerts us to the mistakes that we should avoid. He describes cultural shifts that affect our witness, even the more recent shift in the West toward postmodernism and the challenges it presents.

For readers who are not familiar with Michael Green, some things may be mentioned. He attended colleges at Oxford and Cambridge. During his years as a student, he nurtured his evangelical convictions and developed his bold yet winsome evangelistic style. He engaged in personal evangelism as well as public apologetics. While at Oxford, he was president of the Oxford University Christian Union. He tells us of the events in 1954, when a small group of Christians took a risk and invited a young evangelist from America to hold meetings in London's Harringay Arena. The venue was packed nightly with people to hear Billy Graham of North Carolina.

A few years later, Michael witnessed firsthand the lasting fruit of the Harringay Arena meetings. It was after his first pastorate, when he worked as a tutor at London College of Divinity, that Michael met several students who had come to faith while hearing Billy Graham. Michael also tells us of the friendships that formed. Graham's primary assistant at the Harringay Arena was none other than John Stott. Michael and Stott remained friends for the rest of their lives.

In 1967, Michael was invited by Stott and J. I. Packer to speak at a gathering of evangelical leaders at the National Evangelical Anglican Congress. Two years later Michael became principal of London College of Divinity. During this time, he wrote two books that established him as a well-known evangelist and apologist, *Man Alive* (1967) and *Runaway World* (1968).

In 1975, Michael became Rector of St. Aldate's Church in Oxford, as well as chaplain of the Oxford Pastorate. This was a strategic place for him to serve—in a parish where student ministry was paramount and opportunities for evangelism were abundant. His pace of ministry was demanding. Despite several challenges, Michael developed ministries to equip students and laity for evangelistic witness.

One often assumes that evangelists spend all their time preaching the gospel. Not so; they equip Christians for evangelism. The apostle Paul writes, "So Christ himself gave the apostles, the prophets, *the evangelists*, the pastors and teachers, *to equip his people for works of service*, so that the body of Christ may be built up" (Ephesians 4:11–12). Evangelists do not simply preach the gospel; they train others to proclaim the gospel. Evangelists do this by modeling evangelism, by going before us and creating opportunities for us to engage in evangelism. Michael was this kind of evangelist—in his gospel preaching, in his modeling of evangelism, and in his equipping Christians to share the good news. He carried out this ministry in the parish and the academy.

In 1987, Michael and his wife, Rosemary, relocated to Canada where he was professor of evangelism at Regent College in Vancouver. It was said that his classes touched students' hearts, minds, voices, and feet. The students shared the gospel with their words and by their actions. Michael organized evangelistic missions in cities in British Columbia and Washington state. Just as he had taken students from his congregation at St. Aldate's in England on outreach missions, he took Regent students with him into the streets. Instruction about evangelism in the classroom was a prelude to practicing it in local neighborhoods. When invited to teach a course on evangelism at Fuller Seminary in California, he organized his class to hold an outdoor meeting at Pasadena City College that included dance, drama, music, and testimony.

This practice of "on the job" teaching continued right up until the end of his life. During his last decade, Michael played a key role in the Fellowship of Evangelists in the Universities of Europe (FEUER). Through this network, he traveled to and spoke at university missions across Europe, accompanied by young staff and students who learned from his example. They were regularly amazed at his energetic enthusiasm—not just in preaching but also in accompanying students on the campus in order to hand out flyers and engage in conversations with those he met. Michael once commented to his friend, Lindsay Brown, "I want to die with my boots on!" Michael invested in the younger generation right up to the end of his life.

When I think of Michael Green, I am reminded of August Hermann Francke (1663–1727), a professor of theology in Halle, Germany. Francke took his students with him to the neighborhood of Glaucha known for its beer huts, dance houses, drunkenness, and prostitution. Along with his students, he shared the gospel with people in the streets and held Bible studies in pubs and local apartments and saw spiritually lost people convert to faith. Similarly, Michael modeled evangelism and nurtured within his students a passion for gospel witness while sharpening their evangelism skills.

In *Evangelism: Learning from the Past*, Michael introduces us to Christians known for their evangelistic passion, people we can learn from today. Certainly, while some methods may not be transferable, others are useful (and some should be avoided altogether). Nearly all of the evangelists selected from history—like those of the first century—displayed a passion for "chattering the message" (*lalountes to logon*). Michael highlights the creativity of some evangelists in their cultural contexts. In the case of Patrick of Ireland, this well-known saint employed a strategy of "belonging before believing" that remains useful today. Moreover, Patrick used poetry, song, art, and nature, which tapped into right-brain faculties of intuition, emotions, and imagination, drawing Celts into hearing the gospel story. Michael invites readers to consider this pattern as well, and this is something he modeled in his own ministry, as mentioned above.

It is acknowledged that evangelists of history had shortcomings. They were sinner-saints used by God. Michael was certainly aware of their failures, weaknesses, and in some cases injustices, especially when examined by contemporary sensibilities and standards. Unexpectedly, Michael died before this book could be edited. His words have remained unchanged from his original draft. Therefore, an editorial footnote has been added to point out an area that could have been addressed had he been alive to do so.

Michael Green exhibited a gift of distilling the complex into the understandable. In this book, he helps us understand gospel witness from the perspective of evangelists of history in a way that is easy to follow and comprehend. He shows us how God used ordinary Christians to have extraordinary impact for the gospel when they yielded their hearts, hands, and voices to him.

Introduction

Everyone needs a goal in life. Last night I saw a BBC program about a man whose whole purpose in life was to produce the largest gooseberries. My purpose in life has been to pass on, as best I can, good news. It is the best news anyone could ever hear: that there is a living God, who cares enough about us to become one of us, who dealt at great personal cost with the evil in the world, who is alive to make us into a renewed community, and who invites us to share his home after death. This is the message of the Bible: it is a magnificent message, and I have made sharing it with others the great passion of my life. I have done so by preaching God's good news in every inhabited continent, by seeking (very imperfectly) to conform my life to it, and by using not only preaching, personal conversation, and debate, but radio, TV, and books in the cause of evangelism.

I had already written quite extensively about spreading the good news of the gospel: *Evangelism in the Early Church*, *Evangelism through the Local Church*, *Evangelism Now and Then*, *Sharing Your Faith with a Friend*, *When God Breaks In*, and *Compelled by Joy*. In this book I have set out to trace some of the path from Jesus to the present day and to highlight some of the most effective evangelists. The final chapter details some of my own experience, since I believe nobody should write about evangelism without doing it. Inevitably I have sometimes incorporated material from my previous books.

Be clear what this book is not. It is not a concise, systematic history of evangelism. It is not complete, but selective. It is not comprehensive, but majors on the evangelical tradition and particularly its outworking in Britain.

Be equally clear what it is: merely one man's perspective on this great story of evangelism, with the hope that it will lead the reader to reflect on the past and resolve to take the good news of Jesus into future passionate outreach.

1

Evangelism, Jesus Style

Jesus of Nazareth is God's good news in person, and he has been recognized as such by the worldwide church down twenty centuries. So any attempt to encapsulate the good news that Jesus embodied is sure to be inadequate to do him justice. Nevertheless, there are significant elements in his ministry, life, death, and resurrection that stand out and have become a pattern for his followers to seek to emulate. In what follows we shall look at some of these.

In one sense the gospel or good news that Jesus embodied and proclaimed burst on the world with all the suddenness of an invasion. Mark grasps this well in his opening words about Jesus: "After John was put in prison, Jesus went into Galilee, proclaiming the good news of God. 'The time has come,' he said. 'The kingdom of God has drawn near. Repent and believe the good news'" (1:14–15). It was unexpected for a number of reasons, but particularly because the prevalent Jewish hope and expectation was of a royal figure of King David's line who would forcibly deliver Israel from her enemies—in this case, from their Roman overlords. And Jesus came from a humble working-class family in Nazareth, an insignificant village, and had no militaristic intentions.

When the Time Was Ripe . . .

But in another sense, the good news that Jesus embodied had a long history. It began not on Christmas Day but two millennia earlier with God's gracious covenant with Abraham, and his promise that in Abraham's descendants all the world would be blessed. Abraham's descendants, the Jewish people, repeatedly failed to be a blessing to the world, but at last one of them became just that, a blessing to the whole world, and today around a third of the world profess to follow him. The entire history of Israel finds its fulfillment in him. He is the ultimate priest, the ultimate sacrifice, thus eclipsing the sacrificial system so central to Israel. He is David's son and also his Lord. He is the suffering servant of whom Isaiah spoke, and the glorious Son of Man, raised after terrible suffering to God's right hand (Daniel 7:13). In images like this the way was prepared for Jesus, as Malachi had said it would be (3:1). And the message was reinforced by John the Baptist, the last and greatest of the prophets, who proclaimed the coming of the Savior.

What is more, the world situation was just right for the coming of Jesus and his unique message. Three factors combined. First, there was the Greek language. Alexander the Great had conquered most of the known world, and one of his goals was to bind the whole world together through the use of the Greek language. He largely succeeded. The Greeks also brought to the world a quest for truth and wisdom through the work of their great philosophers, and the Christian faith benefited enormously from this linguistic and intellectual inheritance. Second was the Roman peace. After nearly a century of civil war, practically the whole known world was under the control of Rome, and Rome was, since 27 BC, dominated by an emperor. The first of these emperors, Augustus, made sure that the rule of law was established and that communications were easy through the magnificent road system and through the elimination of piracy so that sea travel was fairly safe. Third, of course, was the Jewish faith, with its strong belief in one God, faithful to his people, utterly just and yet full of love and mercy, a God who demanded holy living in his people. Ever since the northern kingdom of Israel had been carried off in the eighth century BC, Jews had spread (and prospered) worldwide, so their faith was well known even if most people regarded it as very strange. But Jewish faith, Roman roads and justice, and Greek language and culture all combined as never before or since, to prepare the world for the spread of the good news that Jesus would bring.

What, then, were some of the key elements in the good news that Jesus brought and embodied?

Features of the Good News

First and foremost was his authoritative teaching. He "taught with authority and not like the scribes"—the clergy of the day (Mark 1:22). They would laboriously quote authorities who had preceded them. He never did that, but just gave them his message, often prefaced by "Truly, truly I tell you"— something unprecedented in any previous teacher. The essence of his message was that the kingdom of God was upon them. This did not mean a physical realm: the word means primarily "kingly rule." It means the time when God breaks in to establish his royal rule, a red-hot topic in his day. Every Jew was on tiptoe waiting for God to do just that. The trouble was they all had different ideas of how it would come to pass. The Sadducees were the aristocratic party, and they were very much in bed with the Roman overlords: they hoped that this would eventually bring in the kingdom. Their opponents, the Pharisees, reckoned that if Israel could keep the whole law for a single day, that would bring in the kingdom. The zealots, who were committed to violent revolution, chipped away at

Roman rule by killing the odd one off on a dark night and by periodic revolutions that were put down with massive Roman savagery. Then there were the Covenanters—as scholars call them because they lived according to a community rule, or covenant—in their desert refuge at Qumran. They kept to themselves but were determined to fight when God's great day appeared. So it was a time of massive expectation and a variety of suggested methods.

It was into this tinderbox of anticipation that Jesus dropped his spark: the kingdom of God has drawn near! And as he continued his teaching, he made it abundantly clear that he was showing what God's kingly rule looked like, embodying it, and furthering it. The message was sharpened by a unique and stirring call: men and women were to repent of the evil in their lives and follow him—not follow the law or the temple, central though these were to Judaism, but him. For he was the kingdom in himself. This powerful, explosive teaching, with its challenge to personal response to himself, is perhaps the most distinctive and amazing element in the way Jesus sought to bring in the kingdom.

But Jesus's proclamation was matched by his deeds. This caused amazement from the very start of his ministry. In the first chapter of Mark, the oldest Gospel, we read, after a powerful exorcism, "The people were all so amazed that they asked one another, 'What is this? A new teaching—and with authority! He even gives orders to evil spirits and they obey him'" (1:27). The power of his exorcisms is stressed in the Gospels: the writers realize that this is a battle between the kingly rule of God and the rebel rule of Satan, and they do not hesitate to say so, time and again. Whether we look at the demons of Mark's Gospel or the satanic temptations of Matthew and Luke or the usurper "prince of this world" in St. John, it is made clear that the proclamation of good news stirs up the wrath and power of evil forces, but that, despite appearances, they do not prevail.

Another aspect of Jesus's deeds that caused such amazement, joy in the recipients, and wrath among the authorities was his healing of a variety of illnesses, many of them on the Sabbath day. He was demonstrating God's desire for wholeness and healing in his people, whether it was leprosy, lameness, blindness, paralysis, or deafness. In addition, there were instances when he exercised God's power over nature, causing storms to cease or a handful of loaves to feed five thousand. There can be no doubt that he both proclaimed the kingly rule of God and demonstrated it. That was his good news.

An utterly amazing feature about Jesus and his good news project was this: unlike any great leader before or since, he actually practiced what he preached. Socrates did not do that. Muhammad certainly did not. Nobody but Jesus set a perfect example of servant leadership unmarred by any failings. "I have given you an example," he said, "that you should do as I have done for you" (John 13:15). Nobody will listen to a preacher whose life belies his profession.

Another of his notable characteristics was his compassion. When overprotective disciples tried to shoo children away from their master, he invited them to come to him and even dandled one or two of them on his lap. When he saw an old widow throwing her day's livelihood into the collection, he marveled at her self-sacrifice. When an unknown woman crept into a meal and anointed him prior to his death, he said that this deed would be known all round the world—as it has been. When he saw the distress of Martha and Mary at Lazarus's tomb, he wept with them. Here was no strong, authoritarian preacher with remarkable powers but someone who was compassionate and loving to all.

Another feature of Jesus, the bringer of good news, was this: he had a passionate concern for justice. All through the Old Testament, particularly in the Prophets, it is emphasized that God cares about justice and exercises his power on behalf of the poor and needy. We see precisely the same in the attitude of Jesus.

CHAPTER 1

He is furious with the crooked leaders who "devour widows' houses," and, in a very telling passage in Matthew's Gospel, he offers a scathing denunciation of the Pharisees and teachers of the law (23:13–38). Have a look at it and ask yourself if anybody concerned for justice ever dared to speak so powerfully and so directly against the abuses of his day. Sadly, the passion for justice does not always characterize modern evangelists.

A very significant thing that strikes me about the way Jesus went about the good news business is the priority he gave to training a team. He was not a solo operator like most Old Testament prophets. He gathered around him twelve very ordinary men, and he selected them as representatives of the new kingdom of God. He took them with him everywhere and trained them, not in a college like the rabbinic schools but on the job. He loved them and poured himself into them. Often they did not understand. Often they were recalcitrant. But he persisted with them, and after his day there was a magnificent band of men and women ready to carry the good news forward.

Finally, of course, Jesus offered himself up as a sacrifice for the benefit of all who would avail themselves of it. He did not merely proclaim the good news. He lived it and he died for it. His voluntary, sacrificial death was the culminating climax of his life. But that was not the end of the story. He rose again and energized the first apostles for a ministry that became worldwide.

That is one way of looking at how Jesus shared the good news of the kingdom. There is another way of looking at it: not so much what he did but what he was.

The Characteristics of Jesus as Good News

First, I notice his confidence. He knew God was his "Abba," his dear Father. You can't evangelize if you do not have confidence in who you are. Otherwise, you are always looking to what others think of you.

Second, he was visionary. Karl Marx ended his Communist Manifesto with the words, "You have a world to win." That was precisely Jesus's vision. Unless you have a clear aim, you will never succeed in effectively passing on the good news.

Third, he was fully aware of spiritual battle: it was not just the hostile religious authorities that he faced but the dark and hostile spiritual forces behind them. In Africa and Asia, evangelists are almost always aware of this. In the West, we are often blind to it, and as a result we are ineffective because we are defeated before we start.

Fourth, Jesus was heavily involved with the public. He did not hide away in books and colleges but was a familiar figure on the hillsides, in the streets, and in the temple. Public acts of kindness and generosity were central to his kingdom purpose.

Fifth, he was fearless in proclamation. Note his clarity, the consuming interest and gripping power of his words, his brilliant illustrations, his combination of depth and simplicity, his meeting people where they were and starting at that point to bring God in, his flexibility, his challenge to decide. All are magnificent qualities for evangelists to seek to emulate.

Sixth, he was intentional in personal conversations. Think of the woman at the well, of Nicodemus, Zacchaeus, or the rich young ruler. One of the best ways to spread the gospel is for one who knows and loves it to spend time and talk with one who does not.

Seventh, Jesus was a trainer of others. He believed in team ministry. He did not operate solo but selected, trained, and cared for a team who loved God, loved people, and were willing to learn.

Eighth, he was prepared to debate. The Gospels are full of Jesus debating with people—religious people, secular people, hostile people, poor people, highly placed people. His knowledge of Scripture, his understanding of people, and his brilliant use of question and repartee often discomfited his opponents but brought delight to the crowd. Evangelists need to be willing, and equipped, to debate the faith in the public square.

Ninth, he was endued with spiritual authority. As we have seen above, the sheer power of this man made an indelible impression. "If I by the finger of God cast out demons, then the kingdom of God has come among you" (Luke 11:20). Evangelists today need to take this note of spiritual power to heart. We need to learn from the Pentecostals the use of exorcism and confident prayer for healing, and from the Catholics the sheer power of worship to reach areas impervious to words.

Finally, his motivation was paramount. This remains important today. All true evangelism springs from motivation. Note how that little word "must" governed his life: "I must do the work of him who sent me while it is still day"; "I have other sheep from another flock, and them also I must bring"; "The good news must be proclaimed to the whole world"; "The Son of Man must suffer" (John 9:4; 10:16; Matthew 28:19–20; Luke 9:22). Jesus was totally constrained by this "must." His ministry did not spring from duty but from passion, passion to do the Father's will. There is no higher motivation than this.

For Reflection

1. Is my proclamation fearless or constrained by political correctness? Is my ministry marked by compassion and concern for justice as well as talk?
2. Do I seek to introduce individuals to Christ in personal conversations?
3. Am I a good team member?
4. Can I endure hard times, opposition, and suffering?
5. Does my lifestyle commend the gospel?

2

Evangelism in the New Testament Church

After reflecting for more than fifty years on the amazing phenomenon of evangelism by the first Christians, four elements particularly stand out for me.

The first is the way in which Jesus, who proclaimed and embodied the kingdom of God, becomes the one proclaimed. The preacher, so to speak, becomes the message. Jesus proclaimed the advent of the kingdom of God. His followers do not appear to have said much about the kingdom, but they had a great deal to say about the king. This is an astonishing thing. The heart of their message was not an ethical system such as you might find in Socrates and Plato; not a religious program, such as we see in Buddhism; but the unashamed and emphatic proclamation of the person who, they believed, had brought into the world the kingly rule of God in a unique fashion and would one day consummate it at the conclusion of all history. They explode all over the ancient world with their message concentrated on Jesus, whose death dealt with human shame and guilt and whose well-attested and glorious resurrection opened the door that had been locked since the death of the first man, and, as they put it, "brought life and immortality to light" (2 Timothy 1:10).

The second astonishing feature that confronts us is the utter transformation of these men and women. They had run away, in fear for their lives, when Jesus was arrested. After his crucifixion in abject disgrace, we might have imagined that they would be even more fearful. But not a bit of it. They are prepared to stand in the most public places and shout out their good news that God had come to the rescue of humanity through the life, death, and resurrection of Jesus. They are prepared to contend with the leadership of their country, the Jewish Great Sanhedrin, no less, and tell them they were wrong about Jesus and that God had reversed their verdict by the resurrection. They are prepared to face opposition, imprisonment, persecution, and death in the prosecution of their task. It is a shattering change from the eleven cowering in the upper room after Jesus's execution.

The third thing that strikes me most forcibly is that they called for a complete and exclusive change of allegiance. People must repent and commit themselves exclusively to worship and obey the crucified and risen Messiah who is Lord of the world. This was unheard of in antiquity. Your average Greek would cheerfully worship a variety of deities. He did not regard belief as important so long as the cult was performed. He did not think religion had anything to do with ethics. And he would certainly regard the exclusive claims Christians made on their members as very strange. Why, they were expected to belong body and soul to Jesus who was called their master (Greek *despotēs*) and was said to have redeemed them from alienation into his own company! So, for the gentile this meant conversion *to* a new faith; for the Jew it meant conversion *within* the faith in which they had been brought up, of which Jesus was now seen to be the summit and goal. But this was extremely difficult for both gentile and Jew to accept, as we shall see below. For both Jew and gentile the scandal of conversion was absolute.

The fourth thing that stands out from even a cursory glance at the New Testament is the astonishing power and courage of these untrained lay evangelists. You could arrest them and forbid them to preach, but on their release they preached all the more passionately. You could throw them into prison, and at times they would convert the jailer. You could kill off their leaders, and others would take their places. It was not only their passion but their mobility that was so remarkable. Making excellent use of Roman roads and ships, they penetrated into Syria, Central Asia Minor, Egypt, and Rome itself, establishing little groups of believers as they went. The impact of their preaching, and their personal evangelistic conversations, was enormous. The movement spread like wildfire and within a generation could be found in every major city of the empire. This was not due to any carefully considered strategy. They would tell you that it was produced by God's Holy Spirit who had been active in Jesus and was now continuing his ministry through his followers. Jesus had promised that his Holy Spirit would be given them and would empower them to proclaim the message worldwide. It happened. This divine Spirit manifested himself in various ways. He gave them boldness (Acts 4:31). He empowered their preaching (1 Thessalonians 1:5). He worked signs and wonders through them as he had through Jesus (Acts 8:6-8; 11:27-28; 14:10). He called out missionaries and evangelists from among them (Acts 11:1-3; Ephesians 4:11). He gave powerful spiritual gifts to the disciples (1 Corinthians 12-14) And the Holy Spirit guided them as they carried out their mission. Acts 16:6-10 is a classic example of this guidance. This new movement was like a forest fire. It was unquenchable. And the missionaries themselves were clear that this was not their power but the power of God's Holy Spirit.

Gentile Opposition

Not surprisingly, such bold and revolutionary proclamation by preachers who had no credentials (apart from God's) aroused massive opposition from a variety of sources. Sophisticated Greeks poured scorn upon their message. St. Paul conceded that to the Greeks the gospel is folly. It is well illustrated by the derision heaped on Paul's Areopagus address by many of those attending.

There is a splendid little graffito found in the palace on the Palatine Hill in Rome that illustrates this scorn from a somewhat later date. It is a picture of a boy with hand upraised in worship, standing before the figure on a cross of a man with an ass's head. Underneath is scrawled "Alexamenos worships his God." Below it is another inscription, written in a different hand. It reads "Alexamenos is faithful." This graphically illustrates the scorn felt even by imperial page boys for this new faith, and the lively Christian reaction. Greeks believed that wisdom resided in general maxims and truths: Christians were claiming that ultimate truth was to be found in a particular event, and a sordid one at that. No wonder there was opposition.

Ordinary run-of-the-mill pagans at Athens thought that the preaching of Jesus and his resurrection were a couple of gods, Jesus and Anastasis (the Greek word for "resurrection"). They were intrigued. In Lystra, a town right out in the bush, they initially honored Paul and Barnabas as Zeus and Hermes, a couple of gods who had, in their mythology, made a previous visit to their city. The locals brought out bulls and wreaths as sacrificial offerings. Of course, the apostles would have none of it. But their message in an idolatrous culture was often seen as an insult to the local gods and provoked intense hostility. An example of this was the riot in the great theater at Ephesus when fury against the Christians was whipped up by the makers of silver shrines to the goddess Artemis, and Paul barely escaped with his life. Hostility was much more common than welcome!

Jewish Opposition

There was opposition from the Jews, too. Because of a series of historical accidents, Judaism enjoyed a protected legal status. And here were these worshippers of a failed messiah trying to shelter under it! As we have seen, Judaism expected a conquering military leader who would expel the Roman overlords. But Jesus had not only failed to do anything of the kind but had been crucified, a fate which, according to the Old Testament, showed that he was under God's curse. These Christians were heretics who had no respect for circumcision, the law, and the temple, all of which were crucial to Judaism. No wonder they violently opposed the Christians. Pisidian Antioch, Iconium, and Lystra provide examples in Acts of this passionate Jewish hatred and persecution of the Christians.

Roman Opposition

But by far the most serious opposition to the new faith came from the great world power, Rome. To begin with, Christians were seen as just one of several sects in Judaism and as such given legal protection. This happens again and again in Acts, notably in Philippi and Corinth. But by the time 1 Peter was written, we see two kinds of opposition emerging. One is social, as 1 Peter 3 makes clear. Christians were deemed antisocial and perhaps already they were being slandered for cannibalism, eating Christ's body and drinking his blood, as they certainly were not long after. But the scene darkens after 4:12, and it looks as if Peter had just heard of the deliberate persecution raging in Rome. The emperor Nero was trying to deflect rumors that he had himself engineered the great fire of Rome in AD 64 that destroyed vast swathes of the city. Perhaps he wanted more space for his gardens? Nero needed a scapegoat and found one in the Christians, unpopular for reasons already stated. Tacitus, the great historian of the early empire, does not believe for a moment that the Christians were guilty, but he records their horrendous sufferings at the hands of the imperial authorities.

Although this persecution seems to have been confined to Rome at the time, the possibilities for enlarging it were now always open. Provincial governors, using Roman case law, could look to the Roman pogrom as a precedent if they so wished—or else ignore it if they chose. This accounts for the spasmodic and irregular pattern of persecutions in the first two centuries. However, the Christians were now very suspect. They would not swear to the Roman gods and they maintained that their Lord was not Caesar but Christ. This led to persecution and death, sometimes for individuals such as Paul in the first century, individual cases under Trajan in the early second century, and Bishop Polycarp a few years later. But at times it erupted into savage persecution, such as the Scillitan martyrs and Diocletian's final bid to rid the world of the "pale Galilean" (as Swinburne later said) in the early fourth century. It was no easy thing to be a Christian in the days of the early church. The same is true in many places today.

In the face of this opposition, which tended to intensify until the accession of Constantine in AD 312, what was it that made the Christian gospel so attractive that it took root all over the known world?

The Appeal of the Gospel

It is plain from the New Testament that the greatest success of the gospel was among the gentile adherents of the synagogue. They had already been attracted by the noble monotheism of the Jews. It made far more sense than the polytheism of the day, which told of endless struggles, jealousies, and love affairs among the immortals. But they had no intention of joining Judaism—it would involve circumcision for all their males, an obscure sacrificial system, and worship at Jerusalem. So when the gospel broke down barriers between Jew and gentile (all were sinners and all were objects of God's mercy) and declared that temple worship, circumcision, and joining a despised, subject race were unnecessary, this was very attractive.

There were two associated factors. One was the sense of increasing political and social disenchantment that was felt by the vast slave population, the lonely, and the maimed. No amount of sacrifice could eradicate it. In the early empire, as shown in the poems of Horace and Vergil, there was enormous relief that a century of civil war had been ended. Augustus was hailed as "savior of the world," and on his coins you would read "The divine Caesar, son of a god." But this euphoria soon faded, as the opening chapters of Tacitus's *Histories* make plain. The Stoic philosopher Epictetus observed, "Caesar can give peace from war but he cannot give peace from sorrow." Rome itself was filthy and overcrowded. Moral degradation was proceeding apace. Life for most people in the first century was, as Thomas Hobbes would later exclaim, "nasty, brutish, and short."

The other factor was the longing for immortality. The mystery religions tried to cater for this widespread hunger. They were secret societies that filled the gap left by the decline of traditional Roman religion and held out to their worshippers the hope of salvation. By the exact performance of sacred ceremonies, they were deemed to be "born again to eternal life" (*renatus in aeternum*). They originated in the East and grew out of age-old fertility rites and nature worship. The worshipper sought divine aid to enrich his life now and guarantee it after death. But these mysteries were expensive to join, irrational, and nonethical. Nobody attempted to show how the death of a bull, in Mithraism, or the bacchic frenzy of the Orphics could make a person sure of salvation. Nobody expected the worshipper to live a better life as a result. The Christian gospel was far more attractive. They could explain how forgiveness was possible through the death of the God-man on the cross. They could meet the hunger for immortality based on the historically attested resurrection. The new life necessitated a new lifestyle, but the Holy Spirit was available to help them. And converts were welcomed into a close-knit society, a bit like the mysteries, that had a sacred washing and a sacred meal and where all members were equal. But unlike the mysteries, the gospel community was open to all. The old distinctions between Jews and Greeks; senators, citizens, and slaves; barbarians and civilized were abolished. No wonder the gospel progressed.

Some of the sophisticated classes, too, found Christianity attractive. There were several reasons. One was the move among thinking people toward monotheism under the influence of Plato and Aristotle. Another was the combination in Christianity of ethics with religious devotion. A third was the spiritual power these people had—witness the impact made by Paul and Barnabas on the governor of Cyprus (Acts 13:4–12). But perhaps the greatest impetus was dissatisfaction with the results of philosophy. Seneca gives us a good insight into the hunger found in even the best first-century philosophers, the Stoics. First, he is increasingly aware of the power of evil, which philosophy cannot cure: "Evil has its seat within us, in our inward part" (*Epistles* 57). And second, his philosophy left no room for immortality. So in his later life he wrote to his friend Lucilius, "It pleased me to inquire into the eternity of souls, or rather to trust in it. I surrendered myself to that great hope. I was beginning to be weary of myself, to despise the fragments of a broken life" (*Epistles* 102). Perhaps there was not such a great difference between the ignorant devotee of the mysteries and the sophisticated philosopher; both were looking for salvation, here and hereafter.

The gospel seems to have made a great, but not overwhelming, impact among Jews, although of course the apostles and all the early converts came from Judaism. Nevertheless, it held great attractions for the Jew. It abolished the sectarian divisions prevalent in Judaism. It met the age-old question, "How can a man be right with God?" by showing that nobody could measure up to divine perfection but that the hope of Habakkuk had come good: a person could be justified by faith in what Christ had done for him. He could be put entirely in the right with God through the cross of Christ, something impossible through Jewish sacrifices, and something central to the evangelism of St. Paul. Moreover, as both Paul and Peter were to emphasize, Isaiah's ancient prophecy of the suffering servant had been fulfilled in Jesus. There were no other candidates! And we can see from the Letter to the Hebrews that the message of Jesus as the ultimate sacrifice, abolishing the sacrificial system, and as the ultimate high priest, uniquely equipped to reconcile God and man, could intelligently be maintained and backed up from the Jewish Scriptures themselves. This was good news indeed for thoughtful Jews.

These are some of the reasons why the gospel made such a great and immediate impact despite the intense opposition it aroused.

Evangelistic Methods

It remains to ask ourselves what were the methods employed by these first Christians to further their message? Our minds would turn naturally toward preaching, and to be sure, public proclamation to large numbers of people can be found in the early pages of Acts, particularly on the festival of Pentecost. But we find to our surprise that public preaching of this sort seems to have played little part in the advance of the gospel. The Roman authorities were very twitchy about large meetings that could become dangerously political, and we do not find much in the way of public preaching such as marked the day of Pentecost until the end of the second century. It might be argued that Philip seems to have been involved in a major revival based on preaching, healing, and exorcism in Samaria, but Samaria was not under direct Roman rule as Judaea was. However, Christians made up for it by bold proclamation in smaller gatherings, initially in the synagogues. Paul's policy was always to go first to the Jews and then to the gentiles. Acts is full of proclamation of this sort. The missiologist Roland Allen has pointed out four characteristics of this synagogue preaching. First, Paul is conciliatory to the susceptibilities of his audience. Second, he is courageous in proclaiming unpalatable truths. Third comes respect for his hearers, their intellectual power and spiritual needs. And fourth, there is an unhesitating confidence in the truth and power of the message, and there is a fearless determination to drive it home.

Although big public meetings were hazardous, the first Christians made as much use of public proclamation as they could. Think of Paul at the Areopagus, before Felix and Agrippa, and in Rome itself (Acts 17, 26, 28). Moreover, in the warm Mid-East climate, much of this naturally took place in the open air, particularly as the first Christians owned no buildings. Sometimes, of course, they were able to hire or borrow suitable buildings, and we find Paul making excellent and prolonged use of this facility in the work he did in the School of Tyrannus in Ephesus. But much of it took place in the open air. Acts records evangelism of this kind in Jerusalem, Samaria, Lystra, and Athens. It continued, as we shall see in the next chapter, well into the succeeding centuries.

Personal conversation was probably the main way in which the message spread. Luke highlights it with the story of Philip and the Ethiopian official in Acts 8, and another example is Paul's witness to Sergius Paulus (Acts 13:4–12). We read that the believers, scattered from Jerusalem by persecution, went as far as Antioch in Syria *lalountes ton logon* ("chattering the message")—in this case to Jews only, but that restriction was speedily dropped and a strong church, composed of both Jews and gentiles, resulted in Antioch.

Personal testimony is often worth far more than proclamation or even engaging others in profitable conversation. Testimony says, "This is real. It works. I have proved it in my own life." That is powerful. And it is often to be found in the pages of the New Testament. The writers are full of the difference Christ has made to their lives. They break out joyfully, "Thanks be to God for his unspeakable gift," or speak sorrowfully of "sinners of whom I am chief," or joyfully of Christ's powerful deliverance from "the law of sin which dwells in my members" (2 Corinthians 9:15; 1 Timothy 1:15; Romans 7:23). Such personal, passionate testimony almost succeeded in bringing King Agrippa to the feet of Jesus (Acts 26:29).

We find that the first Christians concentrated on the "god-fearing fringe" of the synagogues. This was often quite large. While gentiles drew the line at being circumcised and joining the despised Jewish people, many of them enjoyed Jewish worship, admired their monotheism, and were struck by their Scriptures, which they realized were older than Homer! Acts 13 is a model for preaching where a large proportion of those present are fringe hearers. Paul began where these people were (v. 16), then showed how relevant Scripture was, and that it had come true (vv. 17–23). He told them of God at work in the contemporary situation (v. 25). He preached Jesus, not a doctrine (vv. 38–39), and showed how Jesus could meet their deepest needs that could be met in no other way (v. 39). There was personal testimony (vv. 30–31), an appeal (v. 26), and a warning about the seriousness of the issues involved (v. 41). We may surmise that this sort of thing went on in many a synagogue and bore much fruit—sometimes leading to conversion, as at Corinth where the leader of the synagogue came to faith (18:8).

Another major avenue of their advance was through the home meeting. It went on in Jason's house (Acts 17:5), in Justus's house (17:7), Philip's house (21:8), and so on. Sometimes it was a meeting for prayer (12:12), sometimes a fellowship meal (20:7). Sometimes it was a Communion service (2:42), sometimes an evangelistic day study conference (28:17–28), sometimes a follow-up meeting (5:42) and occasionally they found a house full of seekers (10:22). The sheer variety of these meetings, as recorded in the earliest days of the church, emphasizes the versatile use of the home and the possibility it offered of close personal engagement with individuals. Meetings in a private home had the added advantage of being concealed from prying, hostile eyes, and they could multiply as rapidly as the Christians made their homes available. This was, therefore, an immensely valuable asset, and in the next chapter we shall see how it continued to be exploited in succeeding centuries.

These first Christians were exuberant with the good news that had transformed them, and they loved to discuss it on neutral ground. It might be with Jewish leaders in a hired house in Rome (Acts 28:17–31). It might be when on trial in court (Acts 22 and 2 Timothy 4:16, 17). It might arise from meeting a beggar in the street (Acts 3) or deliberately setting up an occasion for debate and proclamation, as Paul did in the School of Tyrannus. Classic cases are Paul and Barnabas debating and preaching to the ignorant in Lystra, or Paul debating with the intelligentsia in the Areopagus.

The first Christians initiated three other ways of advance that were developed in later centuries, and all of them remain effective today. For one thing, they wrote and used literature. This is evident from the Gospels. Although only John expresses it directly, these all had a mainly evangelistic purpose: "These are written that you may believe that Jesus is Christ, the Son of God, and that by believing you may have life through his name" (John 20:31). The Gospels were supplemented by various written collections, such as apostolic letters, a collection of sayings of Jesus, a collection of the fulfillment of Old Testament prophecies, another on Christian ethical behavior, and another on false teaching. Literature was very important in the spread of the Christian gospel. A second feature was missionary journeys. It is clear from the Acts and the Epistles that these featured prominently in the propagation of the good news. Christians delighted to travel to where Christ was unknown and tell of what he offered people. Third, they planted churches. Church planting remains today the fastest way of spreading the good news, and so it was then. Wherever the preaching led to men and women responding in repentance and faith, these became the nucleus of a new church. That is how the gospel took root so widely in antiquity.

Finally, we need to bear in mind two key principles that seem to have been paramount as they set about the momentous task of reaching the nations. First, they worked outwards from a hot center. They waited, as Jesus bade them, in Jerusalem until they were filled with the Holy Spirit. Only then could they countenance spreading out into Judaea, Samaria, and the ends of the earth. It was the same in Antioch: Barnabas and Saul spent a year and more in building up the church prior to engaging in missionary journeys. It was the same in Ephesus: three years of intensive preaching and teaching so that once the fire was burning brightly the gospel could spread out from that great metropolis to places like Hierapolis and Colossae and other small towns throughout Asia Minor.

Second, and I have deliberately left this to the end because it was so important, they relied on every-member ministry. The spreading of the good news was not confined to apostles and other leaders. It was the job of everyone. Everyone could bear witness to what Christ had done in their lives, though the more structured and in-depth evangelism was doubtless carried out mainly by better-educated Christian leaders, men who have left their imprint on the pages of the New Testament. But there can be no doubt that the main mission of the church was achieved because everyone saw the task of spreading the faith as their responsibility. As the veteran missionary Bishop Stephen Neill put it, "What is clear is that every Christian was a witness. Where there were Christians there would be a living, burning faith, and before long an expanding Christian community." A predecessor of Neill, Adolf von Harnack, in his great work on the expansion of early Christianity, *Mission and Expansion of Christianity*, had declared, "It is impossible to see in any one class of people inside the church chief agents of the Christian propaganda. We cannot hesitate to believe that the great mission of Christianity was in reality accomplished by means of informal missionaries."

For Reflection

1. Does what I proclaim seem good news to those who hear it?
2. Is my message sufficiently challenging to arouse opposition?
3. Does church planting figure on my agenda?
4. Have I built up a believing core that is passionate to reach others?
5. Do I make sufficient use of home meetings, literature, and personal conversations?

3

Evangelism in the
Second to Fourth Centuries

The second and third centuries were marked by the extraordinary advance of the gospel. It spread naturally, often through informal conversations, along the roads and rivers of the Roman Empire. Merchants and evangelists carried the gospel east into Arabia, Syria, and Persia, west through Alexandria along the whole coast of North Africa, and northwards into Pontus, Armenia, Gaul, and Britain. The impact of the good news in the great province of Asia Minor was immense. We are fortunate to have a letter written by Pliny, the governor of Bithynia, to the emperor Trajan in AD 112 recounting the massive growth of Christianity in the province. The numbers were great: they included people of all ages, genders, and social classes. "For this contagious superstition is not confined to the cities only, but has spread through the villages and rural districts." Pompously he boasts of the actions he has taken: "It is certain that temples which had been almost deserted begin now to be frequented; and the sacred festivals, after a long intermission, are again revived; while there is a general demand for sacrificial animals, which for some time past have met with few purchasers" (Pliny, *Letters*, 10.96). It is obvious that the gospel had been spreading like wildfire in the province. This was true, as well, for the whole area round Ephesus, the largest city in Asia. By the end of the second century, you could find Christian churches in every province of the Roman Empire. As Tertullian, an orator and apologist, put it, in a purple passage, "We have filled every place belonging to you: cities, islands, castles, towns, assemblies, your very camp, your tribes, companies, palace, senate, forum! We merely leave you your temples!" (*Book of Apology against the Heathen* 37).

The Impact of Ordinary Christians

It would be a mistake to imagine that all this advance was due to the official pastors and evangelists, though much of it will have been. Celsus, a powerful opponent of Christianity in the mid-second century, gives us a pagan's impression of what was going on:

> We see in private houses workers in wool and leather, laundry workers and the most bucolic yokels, who would not dare to say anything at all in front of their elders and more intelligent masters. But they get hold of the children privately, and any women who are as ignorant as themselves. Then they pour out wonderful statements: "You ought not to heed your father or your teachers. Obey us. They are foolish and stupid. They neither know nor can they do anything really good, but are taken up with mere empty chatter. We alone know how men ought to live. If you children do as we say you will be happy yourselves and will make your home happy too." And if, just as they are speaking, they see one of the school teachers coming, or one of the more educated class, or even the father himself, the more cautious of them flee in all directions, but the more reckless urge the children to rebel. They whisper, "With father and teacher here we can't explain. We don't want to have anything to do with silly, obtuse teachers. They are corrupt and immoral

themselves, and what is more, they inflict punishment on you! So, if you like, leave father and teacher, and come along with the women and your playmates to the women's quarters or the leather shop or the laundry, and you will get the full story." With words like this they win them over. (Origen, *Against Celsus* 3.55)

Such is Celsus's sarcastic dismissal of ordinary Christians spreading their faith. But what a glorious testimony, albeit from a hostile pen, and what a contrast to the highly intellectualized Christianity dispensed today in sparsely occupied churches by well-educated professional clergy!

Did the Sub-apostolic Church Dilute or Even Lose the Gospel?

However, suspicions have been raised in scholarly circles that the glorious message of New Testament days had been diluted into a sort of primitive Catholicism and moralism, while the great truths taught by Paul and John had been lost. Some would even claim that the gospel went into a dark hole only to emerge at the Reformation. Grace, the new birth, justification, sanctification, union with Christ, and other lofty doctrines so dear to the apostles had been jettisoned and replaced by hierarchical government, legalism in ethics, and a Christology that lost interest in the humanity of Jesus.

There is some truth in this, but it is not the whole truth. *The Epistle to Diognetus*, written early in the second century, gives us one of the few examples we have of their evangelistic writing. It is a gem. How about this for a great Christology? "God did not, as one might have imagined, send to men any servant or angel or ruler . . . but the very Creator and fashioner of all things, by whom he made the heavens, by whom he enclosed the sea. This is the messenger he sent them" (*Epistle to Diogne-*

tus 7). Or how about this as an explanation of the cross? "He himself took on him the burden of our iniquities, he gave his own Son as a ransom for us, the holy one for the transgressors, the incorruptible for the corruptible, the immortal for mortals. For what else could cover our sins but his righteousness? In who else was it possible that we, the wicked and ungodly, could be justified, except in the Son of God alone?" (9). Again, "O sweet exchange, O work of God beyond all searching out! O benefits surpassing all expectation! That the wickedness of the many should be hid in a single righteous One, and that the righteousness of One should justify many transgressors!" (9). And how does a man come to Christ and then live out his faith?

> No one has ever seen him, but he has revealed himself. And he has made himself known through faith, by which alone we can see God. He will give this faith to those who love him. And then with what joy do you think you will be filled? Or how will you love him who has so first loved you? And if you love him, you will seek to imitate his kindness. And do not wonder that a man can imitate God. He can if he is willing. . . . He who takes on himself the burden of his neighbour, he who is ready to benefit his neighbour with anything he has—he is an imitator of God. (10)

Nor is this barren self-effort, with which the second-century writers are often reproached. It is the work of the Spirit, "who was from the beginning, who appeared as if new, and was found old, and yet who is born afresh in the hearts of the saints" (11). There is a clear trust in the power of Christ: "God himself has sent from heaven and placed among men the truth, the holy and incorruptible Word, and has firmly established him in their hearts" (7).

It would be wrong to leave this superb little letter without the famous passage about the Christian way of life that so commended their message:

Christians are distinguished from other men neither by country nor language, nor the customs they observe. For they do not inhabit cities of their own . . . but following the customs of the country in respect of clothing, food, and general manner of life, they display to us the remarkable and admittedly paradoxical manner of their citizenship. They live in countries of their own, but only as aliens. As citizens they share in all things with others, and yet endure all things as foreigners. Every foreign land is their fatherland, and every fatherland is a foreign land. They marry, as do all: they beget children, but they do not destroy their offspring. They have a common table but not a common bed. They are in the flesh, but they do not live after the flesh. They pass their days on earth but they are citizens of heaven. They obey the established laws, and at the same time surpass the laws by their lives. They love all men, and are persecuted by all. In short, what the soul is in the body, Christians are in the world. (5)

Christian Lifestyle

A claim like this points us to one of the key elements in the progress of the gospel, the lives of the Christians. It was, in fact, this transformed lifestyle of the Christians that made such an impact on secular society in this period of the church's great advance. Justin, writing in the mid-second century, exclaims,

We who formerly delighted in fornication now embrace chastity alone; we who formerly used magic arts dedicate ourselves to the good and unbegotten God; we who valued above all things the acquisition of wealth and possessions now bring all we have into a common stock, and share it out to all according to their need; we who hated and destroyed

one another, and on account of their different manner of
life would not live with men of another tribe, now, since
the coming of Christ, live happily with them and pray for
our enemies and endeavour to persuade those who hate us
unjustly to live conformably to the good precepts of Christ
so that they may become partakers with us of the same
joyful hope of a reward from God the ruler of all. (Justin,
1 Apology 14)

The link between holy living and effective evangelism could
hardly be made more effectively. The Christians stood out
for their chastity, their hatred of the cruel gladiatorial shows,
their sacrificial good deeds for pagan neighbors, and their
good citizenship. They did not expose their infants or abort
their fetuses. They refused to have anything to do with idolatry even if it meant their execution. Heathen writers of the
day regularly praise their pure lives, devoted love and social
concern, and their amazing courage in the face of opposition.
Here is a moving passage in the second-century writer Athenagoras, describing Christian behavior: "Among us you will
find uneducated people and artisans, and old women who
if they are unable in words to prove the benefit of our doctrine, yet by their deeds show the benefit arising from their
persuasion of its truth. They do not practice speeches but
demonstrate good deeds. When struck, they do not strike
back. When robbed, they do not go to law. They give to those
who ask them, and they love their neighbors as themselves"
(Athenagoras, *A Plea for the Christians* 11).

The Christian writings of the second century are full of
encouragements to holy living. It was essential if people
were to believe the good news the evangelists proclaimed.
Otherwise they would have had no impact. As the writer of
2 Clement put it, "When the heathen hear from our mouth the
oracles of God, they wonder at their beauty and greatness:
then, discovering that our deeds are not worthy of the words

we utter, they turn from their wonder to blasphemy, saying that it is all a myth and delusion" (2 *Clement* 13.1). This strong emphasis on morality in the writers of the second and third centuries underlines for us the truth that the good news must be lived as well as proclaimed. The first Christians succeeded not only because they out-argued but also because they out-lived the pagans.

There was another important element in Christian advance: persuasive proclamation. A lot of it took place in these centuries, and the approach to Jews and gentiles was very different.

Christian Apologetic to Jews

It is clear from the New Testament that Paul and other missionaries went first to the Jews before going on to reach the gentiles. They were God's chosen people, Jesus was the climax of Judaism, and the early missionaries were not going to neglect them. To be sure, Jews were longing for a messiah, an anointed deliverer of their people from gentile domination. As we have seen, there were conflicting expectations of this coming figure. Was he the Son of David? Yes, said the evangelists (hence the importance of the genealogies in their approach), yes but he is David's Lord as well, seated at the Father's right hand (Psalm 110). Was he a political leader? Yes, but not of a physical kingdom: instead, he welded together men and women of all backgrounds into a community under his leadership. Did they look for a prophetic or maybe a priestly messiah? Well, he was both. Everyone recognized Jesus as a prophet, but as the Letter to the Hebrews pointed out, Jesus is also the ultimate high priest. Was he the Son of Man? Once again, the Christians could give a modified "Yes." He was the Son of Man whose glories Daniel (7:14) had reveled in, but he was a suffering Son of Man, something unheard of in Judaism. They emphasized the way Jesus himself had combined the utterly contrasting role of glorious Son of Man and humble suffering servant (Isaiah 53).

In ways like this, the early Jewish evangelists strove to convince their compatriots about the identity of the Jesus they were proclaiming: he was the fulfillment of Israel's Scriptures and Israel's hopes. Determined to convince their hearers, we find them burrowing deeply into the Scriptures. This is evident both in the New Testament itself and in Justin's *Dialogue with Trypho*, a fascinating debate between a Jew and a Christian early in the second century. Of course, the death of Jesus presented a massive obstacle to evangelism. How could he be Messiah if instead of rescuing Israel he had been executed by the Romans? How could he be Messiah if he ended up on a cross, the ultimate mark of God's curse? But the Christians maintained that the cross of Jesus represented not weakness but power: it was there that he met and conquered the forces of evil. He reigned from a tree, as they loved to say. And the proof of this argument that the cross meant not weakness but victory was, of course, the resurrection. This was clearly central in their preaching. As for the objection that the messiah could not have died under a curse, the evangelists agreed that the cross was the place of cursing but maintained that Jesus took the place of cursing in place of the whole world's accursed sin in order to rid us of its burden.

As is evident in the pages of Acts, there was considerable initial success in the Jewish mission. The evangelists seem to have exercised real sensitivity. For instance, nowhere in the Acts sermons is Jesus declared to be God. That might impugn strict Jewish monotheism. But the convictions underlying the categories in which they proclaimed Jesus were much the same: Jesus in the early speeches in Acts does things that are attributed to God in the Old Testament, and he is raised to the throne of the Almighty. Jews were much happier to see

Jesus as the one on whom the Spirit came in all his fullness, as second-century Jewish works like the Gospel of the Ebionites and the Gospel of the Hebrews reveal. Had this more flexible approach to Christology persisted, the early success of the Jewish mission might have been extended. As it was, attitudes hardened on both sides and an insuperable chasm emerged by the 80s of the first century.

The evangelists must have seemed like robbers to the Jews. First, they stole their status as the "Israel of God." Second, they stole their Scriptures, ransacking the Old Testament for texts that they could attribute to Jesus: some Christians, like Justin, maintained that the Jews had entirely forfeited their right to the Old Testament Scriptures. Third, the Christians would have been seen to break Israel's law. They saw the law as leading to Christ, and they were not at all careful to maintain the actual injunctions contained in it, such as food laws and behavior on the Sabbath. Finally, the Jews who did not believe in Jesus as Messiah must have been exasperated by the way the Christians spiritualized their sacred rites. It was a fair complaint. Sabbath, circumcision, temple, sacrifice, and priests were all dispensed with by the early Christians, spiritualized or at best regarded as highly suspicious optional extras. So it is not surprising that on the whole the Jewish mission was something of a failure. In the early days there was success in Judaea, Egypt, Syria, and Rome. The character of Jesus was attractive. The witness of the evangelists to the resurrection was intriguing. The argument from Scripture carried weight, and the joyous fellowship among the Christians, along with the confident offer of pardon, was appealing. But the destruction of the temple and the sack of Jerusalem in AD 70 was portrayed by the Christians as divine judgment on Israel, while the blame for the crucifixion was increasingly placed on the Jews. If ever any evangelistic enterprise taught the lesson that the gospel cannot be preached without love and sensitivity, this was it. The Christian community and their evangelists failed to make it credible to the Jews that they were in fact the community of the Messiah.

Christian Apologetic to Gentiles

By far the greatest success lay in the gentile mission. That, of course, demanded massive retranslation of Jewish language and concepts if they were to be understood by gentiles who despised and misunderstood everything Jewish. So instead of "Messiah," which would have been meaningless to gentiles, or "Son of God," which would merely indicate a hero, we see a move toward the word "Lord." This title is constantly used of God in the Greek Old Testament, the Septuagint. It also made excellent sense in the Hellenistic world. They knew all about Lord Serapis, Lord Osiris, and the rest, but above all the word was used of the emperor. So the title had strong connotations, with the additional hint that Jesus, not Caesar, was Lord of the world. At the same time, it was true to the basic baptismal confession "Jesus is Lord." In the same way "kingdom of God," so common in Jewish thought, would have been completely misunderstood in pagan circles; although it never completely died out, it was increasingly replaced by synonyms such as "salvation" (for which people all over the empire were longing) or "eternal life," which, of course, had great appeal. Another example is the use of "adoption" language. This was unknown in Judaism but significant in Greco-Roman life. What a wonderful way of showing that although we were originally alienated from God, he is willing to receive believers into his very family

Such necessary cultural translations are all to be found in the New Testament itself. But they are very evident in the two centuries that followed. A gap began to open up between the defender of "orthodoxy" who was concerned to maximize the difference between authentic Christianity and all deviations from it, and the apologist and evangelist, who was concerned to minimize the gap and stress the common ground between him and his potential converts. It is with the latter group that we are concerned here. This is what the apologists were trying to do with their defense of the faith, written and spoken—of whom Justin is the prime example. This, too, is what the ordinary evangelists were trying to do, and for several centuries they tended to preface their presentation of the good news by an attack on idolatry, a proclamation of the one true God who had shown himself in Jesus, and an insistence on transformation of life, which inevitably ensues from true conversion.

The apologists, as they are called, had a twofold aim. One was to make the faith intelligible to gentiles, and so they developed the principle of translation explained above. Justin was a secular philosopher converted to Christianity who continued to wear his distinctive philosopher's robe and maintained that Christianity was the true philosophy. He was perhaps the first, after Paul and John, deliberately to reconcile Christianity with Hellenistic thought, and made great play with the idea of the Logos ("Word") which, of course, John had used in his gospel. Reference to the Logos, divine reason, was common in intellectual circles, and Justin argued that before the coming of Christ men had been able to attain bits and pieces of the truth through possessing "seeds" of the divine reason. At Christ's coming, the whole Logos took shape and was made man. So Justin was strong on the incarnation of the Logos but broad in his recognition that there are truths of philosophy as well, which because they are true must be due to the working of the same Logos that was fully manifested in Christ. Later apologists, such as Clement and Origen, built on this same structure. Its strength is its liberal appreciation of secular thought. Its danger is syncretism with non-Christian ideas, something the apologists did not entirely escape.

The second aim of Justin and other apologists was to defend the faith against pagan accusations of various kinds and to commend Christianity as both true and wholesome. These "apologies" (defenses of the faith) were addressed either to the emperor of the day or to provincial governors. Justin was concerned to gain justice for Christians. But whether the emperor or any of the provincial governors ever read this material is highly doubtful. We may doubt whether the apologists made great headway in advancing the faith, though they were certainly very valuable internally within the church in countering the gnostic and other heresies that emerged. There must have been further factors that led to the massive growth of the early church. Two in particular stand out.

Christian Endurance under Persecution

One was the endurance of Christians under persecution. The first persecution was perpetrated by Nero after the great fire of Rome, which he (wrongly) blamed on the Christians. They endured unimaginable tortures that shocked even an aristocratic historian like Tacitus. "Mockery was heaped upon them as they perished," he wrote. "They were covered with the skins of wild animals and torn apart by dogs, or nailed to crosses, or set alight, so that when darkness came they served as torches" (Tacitus, *Annals* 15.44). After Nero's assault, provincial governors had a precedent for persecuting Christians if they wished. Many did not, but sporadic persecutions broke out throughout the period until Constantine's Edict of Toleration in AD 313. The behavior of Christians under torture and execution made a profound impact on those who saw it or heard about it. Three examples paint the picture very clearly.

The first was a celebrated Christian leader, Bishop Polycarp of Smyrna. He was arrested at a great pagan festival in Smyrna in AD 155 and was burned to death at the instigation of a furious mob who shouted out that "This is the teacher of

Asia, the father of the Christians, the overthrower of our gods, he who has been teaching many not to sacrifice or to worship the gods" (*Martyrdom of Polycarp* 12). The governor gave him a chance to recant and worship the pagan gods. Polycarp declined, saying that he had served Jesus for eighty-six years and he had never harmed him, so he was not going to deny him now!

The second example comes from AD 177 when a slave girl, Blandina, herself a recent convert, was tortured with fiendish ingenuity, put on a gridiron, thrown to the beasts in the arena, forced to watch the murder of her Christian companions, then impaled upon a stake—as she prayed for her tormentors. An eyewitness recorded all this in a letter that appears almost in full in the *Ecclesiastical History* of Eusebius.

The third example was Perpetua, aged twenty-two and married a year earlier. With a baby at her breast, she was martyred in AD 203 in Carthage. Before her death she managed to record her impressions of her imprisonment. Her father tried everything to make her recant. First, he was tough with her. Then he turned to appeals—his gray hairs, her mother, and her tiny son were all brought up to get her to change her mind. But she remained firm and went with dignity to her death. The effect of such courageous and principled martyrdoms was enormous. Stoics and others had died with courage, but nobody had seen men and women go to their deaths rejoicing. Such self-sacrifice did much to commend the truth of their gospel and draw others to join them.

Christian Healings and Exorcisms

I have left to last the greatest avenue of gospel advance during this period. It concerns the sheer power of God. It was this that won over vast numbers of ordinary people. This power, adumbrated in the ministry of Jesus and the letters of Paul and attested in the second-century Long Ending of Mark, showed itself not only in heroism but also in healing and exorcism. The classical scholar Ramsay MacMullen has written a fascinating book, *Christianizing the Roman Empire (AD 100–400)*, which demonstrates this very clearly. He quotes Eusebius, the great church historian writing early in the fourth century, who describes the evangelists "planting the saving seed of the heavenly kingdom far and wide in the world, . . . evangelizing . . . with God's favor and help, since wonderful miracles were wrought by them in those times also through the Holy Spirit" (*Ecclesiastical History* 3.37). The apocryphal Acts of John tells of the apostle winning many over through healings, and more still by driving out the demonic power from the great temple of Artemis in Ephesus. The altar split in two, some of the building fell down, and the assembled Ephesians cried out, "There is but one God, the God of John" (Acts of John 42). Although the story is apocryphal, MacMullen shows that it, and similar demonstrations of power, was widely believed in the second and third centuries and led to many conversions. After all, men believed in many gods in those days, and if the gospel was to be shown as superior, why should God not exert his power in such ways? Three sources tell us of the amazing acts of power wrought through Gregory the Wonderworker in the third century. He worked in Pontus, in the city of Neocaesarea, and won over the majority of the population to the faith. On one occasion he spent the night in a temple, mostly in prayer. When he left in the morning, the temple warden turned up only to find that the demon, through which he gave oracular responses to worshippers' questions, had departed, banished by the greater power of Christ. On another occasion while Gregory was preaching, a youth challenged him. Gregory perceived he was demonized, and he exorcised the demon, saying, "Not I is it that commands you but Christ who flung you with the swine into the sea. Quit this youth!"

In fact, exorcism, along with healing, seems to have made the most impact for the gospel. MacMullen scorns the skepticism of historians who make this a "no-go" area. He cites Justin, an early Christian apologist, who boasted, "How many persons possessed by demons, everywhere in the world and in our own city, have been exorcized by many of our Christian men" (*2 Apology* 6). Irenaeus later in that second century writes, "Some people incontestably and truly drive out demons, so that those very persons often become believers" (in Eusebius, *Ecclesiastical History* 5.7.4). Tertullian, a little later, invites skeptics to observe for themselves: "Let a man be produced right here before your court who, it is clear, is possessed by a demon, and that spirit, commanded by any Christian at all, will as much confess himself a demon in truth as, by lying, he will elsewhere profess himself a 'god'" (*Apology* 23). This is all apropos of Tertullian's passionate plea that they should believe in Christ. If his pagan audience is disposed to mock, Tertullian rounds on them: "All the power and authority we have over the demons comes from naming the name of Christ. Thus they become subject to the servants of God and Christ. At our command they leave, distressed and unwillingly, the bodies they have entered. Before your very eyes they are put to an open shame" (*Apology* 23). Again he says, "We do more than repudiate the demons. We overcome them. We expose them daily to contempt and exorcise them from their victims. This is well known to many people." Such claims would be pointless and counterproductive if they were not true. The same emphasis on the extraordinary power of the Christian mission is repeated in Minucius Felix, Tatian, Origen, and the *Apostolic Constitutions*.

These demonstrations of divine power were so undeniable that Jews and pagans tried to use the name of Jesus as a magic charm! But always the emphasis of these evangelists and apologists was not on the miracle itself but on its supporting role in validating the good news of the gospel.

CHAPTER 3

For Reflection

1. Is my proclamation of the gospel marked by love?
2. Do I take pains to study the culture in order to make the gospel persuasive?
3. How seriously do I take the power of the Holy Spirit for impact, in areas such as healing and exorcism?
4. Is my church marked by individuals who love to talk about Jesus?

4

Nominalism, Bishops, and Monasteries

After an intensive three years of persecution by the emperor Decius, ending with his death in battle in AD 251, the last half of the third century saw great growth in the church. Opposition decreased and numbers soared. The social historian Rodney Stark gives good reason for supposing that there was a 40 percent growth rate over these decades, and that by the year AD 300 there were over six million Christians in the empire. But in AD 303 the emperor Diocletian launched a massive assault on the church in the hope of crushing it before it engulfed the empire. By AD 311 opposition had died out, and in the next year Constantine, with the cross emblazoned on the shields of his army, became the undisputed ruler of the Western empire. He was well disposed toward Christians and gave credit for his victory to the Christian God. So in AD 313 he issued the Edict of Toleration. Christianity was now legal, links between church and state were strengthened and, after a couple of years of fierce opposition by the emperor Julian in AD 361–363, we find to our embarrassment that by the end of the century, conversion would be enforced by law for those within the Roman empire.

The accession of Constantine made a massive change for the church, both for good and ill. Hitherto it had survived and flourished amid the disapproval and often opposition of the state. Now all that was gone: it was officially welcomed, and vast numbers flooded into the church. But imperial favor proved more deadly than imperial persecution. The emperor wanted to have a say in church affairs and in fact chaired the famous Council of Nicaea in AD 325. Many of the new church members were manifestly insincere and the problem of nominal attachment without a corresponding faith and lifestyle became acute. Furthermore, Christianity for the first time became associated with war after Constantine had conquered in the name of Christ—a sinister and far-reaching precedent. This dilution of the quality of church life was distressing, and led, among other things, to the rise of monastic communities, as we shall see below. Meanwhile, the church had to adjust to the decay of the Roman empire as pagan tribes began to move into territories previously held by Rome. The church now faced the daunting challenge of seeking to evangelize these barbarian tribes and incorporate them into the church.

Under these circumstances, how was this work of evangelism carried on? In three ways: through the ordinary Christians, the bishops, and the monasteries.

Lay Christian Witness

During the terrible years of the persecution under Decius and Diocletian, many Christians recanted to save their skins. But most did not. Persecution only strengthened the resolve of courageous men and women, and particularly women, to stand fast and to proclaim the good news wherever they could. There were few church buildings until the second half of the fourth century, so the church was very much based in the home and even on the streets. Many Christians were merchants with great opportunities for using the superb Roman road system to their advantage. Most lay Christians continued to take the Great Commission as their mandate for evangelism. Many believed that the return of Christ was imminent, so the time was short. The darkness of the times only served to enhance the urgency of their appeal. Whether in home or marketplace, men, women, and even children were busy chattering the good news. Prayer was paramount. Christians were always praying for the door of opportunity to open, and when it did they went through it. They relied on the leading of the Holy Spirit. When persecution came, they constantly offered hope and forgiveness to their tormentors, who were mired in hatred and revenge. Much of that courageous grassroots outreach must have continued during the reign of Constantine and later, in sharp contrast to the nominalism of many entering the church.

Mercifully, some very great men, mostly bishops with a passion for evangelism, emerged during this period. This is not altogether surprising because the gospel from the very start reached many educated people: it was certainly not merely, as some have argued, the religion of slaves and tradespeople. Just think of Saul of Tarsus, the brightest intellectual star of his generation. The city treasurer at Corinth and the proconsul of Cyprus were Christians. So was Pomponia Graecina, the wife of the governor of Britain, who was tried in AD 57 for following a "foreign superstition." Acilius Glabrio and Flavius Clemens, high-ranking senators toward the end of the first century, were Christians. Clemens's wife, Domitilla, was one of the most important women in the empire, since she was niece of the emperor Domitian and mother of two sons designated to succeed him: she was also a Christian and was exiled for her faith. There were from early days plenty of intellectuals as well, men like Justin Martyr, Tatian, Clement of Alexandria, Origen, and many others. So the emergence of strong leaders for the evangelization of the empire once persecution diminished is not surprising.

Five Evangelizing Bishops

Five distinguished bishops did a great deal to win multitudes to the faith in the century after Constantine.

One was Ulfilas, known as the apostle to the Goths. Born in AD 311 to a Christian family taken captive by the Goths, he was brought up in their midst. In due course he was made bishop and carried on extensive missionary work among the Goths in Romania. But persecution drove him to relocate south of the Danube in Bulgaria, where he continued his missionary work, and he translated the Bible into Gothic, the oldest literary work in any Germanic language.

Another distinguished missionary bishop and contemporary of Ulfilas was Martin of Tours. Martin was the son of an army officer, born in Austria, and had to serve as a cavalry officer but left the army as soon as he could. He managed to lead his mother, but not his father, to faith. He set up a monastery but did not remain a recluse. He was constantly on the road. His reputation as an evangelist and exorcist spread all over Gaul, and he led large numbers to faith. He was chosen as bishop of Tours in AD 371 by popular acclaim and reluctantly accepted it, but he continued to live in a monastery even after he became bishop. But he found Tours a superb center for evangelism and campaigned intensively for the evangelization of the heathen Gauls. His humility and godly life had a great impact, and his fame spread to Britain where several churches were named after him. Indirectly he gave great impetus to the evangelization of Britain.

The third great evangelist-bishop was Ambrose of Milan. He was a civil servant in North Italy, and part of his job was to preserve public order during the much-contested episcopal election in AD 373. It looked as if there was deadlock, and then a child's voice piped up, "Ambrose for bishop," which was taken up enthusiastically by the crowd. He was not even baptized at that point! So, with breathtaking speed he was baptized, ordained and made bishop. He was a great Bible expositor and hymn writer and had extensive dealings with the emperor Theodosius. He is remembered for his outstanding preaching, which won many people to Christ. He even sent a mission to the people living in the Alps. And, of course, it was partly through his intelligent and forceful preaching that Augustine became a Christian.

Augustine, the fourth of the great bishops of the fourth century, was an African, and he emerged as the most distinguished Christian thinker, writer, and apologist since the apostles Paul and John. In the face of the impending sack of Rome and while the Visigoths approached Hippo, he wrote *The City of God*, which would inspire and give hope for a thousand years. But his greatest book was his most personal, the *Confessions*. Here he records the influence of his godly mother Monica, his lustful youth at Carthage, his wrestling with the doctrines of Plato and the Manicheans, and his gradual attraction to the Scriptures and the preaching of Ambrose. He speaks of his spiritual torment as he agonized over the challenge of the gospel, his unwillingness to repent, and then the thunderclap of the scriptural injunction in a garden one day when he picked up the New Testament and read, "Let us behave decently as in the daytime, not in orgies and drunkenness, not in sexual immorality and debauchery, not in dissension and jealousy. Rather clothe yourselves with the Lord Jesus Christ, and do not think about how to gratify the desires of the sinful nature" (Romans 13:13–14). That is how he came to Christ, and in his evangelistic preaching he often referred to it. He founded a small monastery, and in AD 395 he was made bishop of Hippo near his birthplace in Algeria, a post he held for more than thirty-five years, and exercised an enormous influence for the gospel with his preaching, writing, and godly life. We are fortunate in having this wonderful book, the *Confessions*. It reveals many of the elements that combined to win him for Christ: his turbulent and immoral early life, his intellectual journey and success, his inner shame and struggles, the impact of Scripture, his mother's prayers and tears, the preaching of Ambrose, and the death of a close friend. These were all stepping-stones to his commitment to Christ in AD 386. They must have been elements in many of the most solid conversions in his day. They remain frequent elements in conversions nowadays.

But above all they combined to give Augustine an awareness of God's grace antedating his own faith. This precious truth seems to have been dormant in Christian evangelism since the age of the apostles. He was passionate about the sin of man, the cross of Christ, and the sheer grace of God that calls men and women to him long before they ever dream of responding. Great theologian that he was, to whom both Catholics and Reformers look back with gratitude, nothing is more significant in his life and ministry than this insistence on the sheer unmerited grace of God to sinners. And that is the heart of the Christian good news.

Finally, let's savor a little of one of the greatest preachers who ever lived, John Chrysostom. He lived from AD 344–407, throughout the whole of a half century when the ancient world was irrevocably changed. He tried the life of a hermit for a couple of years, but his health suffered and he abandoned it. He became the leading preacher in Antioch, where he had enormous influence among the citizens. It was the happiest period of his life. He was kidnapped and taken off to be bishop of Constantinople in 397, by now the western capital of the empire. He hated the politics that seethed in the capital, but continued his passionate preaching—which often got him into trouble and even exile. He had a huge heart of compassion toward lost people, and this showed up very clearly in his first year as bishop in Constantinople. He had urgent matters on hand—reforming the clergy, organizing church charitable organizations, building hospitals, and maintaining relations with the imperial family. Yet he gave himself to the evangelization of the surrounding countryside and in particular the Goths. He sent missionaries as far as the Black Sea where there was a large colony of Goths. Not only were many of these wild people brought to Christ, but he was able to found the elements of a national clergy among them.

As a preacher he took pains to expound and apply the Scripture with due respect for its historical context. "I cannot let a day pass without feeding you with the treasure of the scriptures," he said. His preaching was relevant, fearless, and very direct as he ministered in two of the most modern cities we could imagine—with poverty, exploitation, immorality, political intrigue, ostentatious wealth all around him, and a lukewarm church very like our own. He castigates the rich women, "Don't you see how great wealth makes people mad? . . . You women who use silver chamber pots should be ashamed. Here is a man made in the image of God, dying of cold and hunger and you are equipping yourselves with such things! . . . Do you so revere excrement that you would receive it in silver? I know you are stunned as you hear this, but it's the women who act like this who should be stunned, and the husbands who pander to them. I won't put up with that excess any more" (*Homilies on Colossians* 7.250). Or listen to his message to the men: "Don't you know that just as we entrust silver to our household slaves, and demand an account of them to the last cent, so does God demand reckoning of the days of our life, how we have spent each day. . . . What excuse shall we make when we come to account? . . . Although you have rented such a great house—I mean this world—from God, you don't pay the rent!" (*Against the Games and Theatres* 265–66). He mingles appeal with challenge, and he is not afraid to mention hell. "Ah, I know you do not like to hear me speak of hell," he says. "Yes, these thoughts are terrible and torture the heart. Do I not know it myself? Do I not feel it as you do? My heart is troubled and palpitates like yours; and the more clearly I understand that hell really exists, the more I shudder and shrink with fear. But I must have the courage to say these things, lest both you and I should fall into that dreaded hell!" (*Homily 9 on First Corinthians*).

Such was the powerful preaching of some of the great leaders in the years following Constantine's Edict of Toleration. Christianity had become the preferred religion in the empire, and its evangelists were free to preach to their heart's content. It had not been like that in the first two centuries, as we have seen. Public preaching was largely out of the question until some periods in the third century, when Irenaeus actively evangelized the pagan tribes near Lyons, and Gregory the Wonderworker gained enormous success in Neocaesarea around AD 240. When he became bishop there were, we are told, only seventeen members in his church; when he died there were only seventeen pagans left in the city! Doubtless an exaggeration, but clearly his evangelism was enormously fruitful.

On the whole, in the first two centuries Christians had concentrated on household evangelism, personal evangelism, and, toward the end of the second century, evangelistic outreach emerging from the great centers of Christian learning in Antioch and Alexandria. Gregory himself was led to Christ by the skilled personal evangelism of Origen, who ran the School at Alexandria, and we have both his and Origen's account of it. As for household evangelism, the large Roman house lent itself to big meetings that could avoid public scrutiny, and the informal atmosphere facilitated discussion and made this sort of evangelism particularly successful. The *Clementine Recognitions*, written toward the end of the second century, give many examples of evangelism of this sort. Someone would hear of an event in a private house and knock. "The master of the house welcomed us and led us to a certain apartment, arranged like a theatre, and beautifully built. There we found considerable crowds waiting for us, who had arrived during the night" (chapter 38). But secrecy was no longer needed after the accession of Constantine, and courageous public evangelism emerged.

Public preaching from strong leaders like these bishops contributed hugely to the spread of the church after Constantine: it built on the household evangelism, personal conversations, and courage in persecution that had proved so effective in previous centuries. And it militated strongly against the nominalism that had entered the church after Christianity became the leading religion in the empire. There was, however, another factor that helped a great deal: the beginning of monasticism.

Monasticism

Monasticism developed as a reaction to the decline in the morals and commitment among church members. This was brought on by the favor extended to the church by most of the emperors after Constantine, thus making it politically expedient to be a Christian. Hence nominalism prevailed in many circles. New adherents maintained their pagan attitudes and lifestyles. This drove many dedicated Christians to seek a purer Christianity in isolated places like desert and mountains.

Monasticism seems to have originated in Egypt, perhaps with the celebrated hermit St. Antony. In AD 285 he gave away all his possessions and retired into the desert. Later he emerged for a while to organize other hermits into a semblance of shared life, but then he retired again to the desert where through his preaching and holy life he acquired great influence. One major motive was escape from the temptations of the world and the corruption of the church, and monasteries multiplied enormously both in East and West for a thousand years. The first monks were usually solitary ascetics, some even living alone on the top of a pillar and preaching to the multitudes who came to see them. But increasingly they moved to monastic communities, which proved very effective in evangelism. The church in the East, increasingly influenced by the Nestorians who maintained that Christ had two distinct personalities, divine and human, were passionate for evangelism and reached throughout Central Asia as far as Azerbaijan and Armenia, India, and China. They were always ready for costly advance, something that became rather less common among the prevailing Catholic Church, particularly in the West. There was, of course, a tension in these early monasteries. The monks wanted on the one hand to escape from the world, but on the other to evangelize it. Consequently, many monasteries were established with the aim of winning people in the surrounding area for Christ, and thousands became Christians through this means. The decline of this evangelistic passion, the loss of the concept of grace, and the emergence of an emphasis on earning merit were unfortunate developments in the Middle Ages. In these later centuries before the Reformation, many monasteries had descended into ignorance, immorality, and greed, although they continued to offer hospitality to travelers and some rudimentary medical care.

Here is an example of the powerful evangelistic preaching given by some of these monks. It comes in the *Spiritual Homilies* of St. Macarius of Egypt, who lived in the early fourth century. It is simple biblical preaching, full of power, and directed to the ordinary non-Christian. "As the woman who was diseased with the issue of blood, on believing truly and touching the hem of the Lord's garment at once found cure, and the flow of the unclean fountain of her blood dried up, so every soul that has the incurable wound of sin, the fountain of unclean and evil thoughts, if it only comes to Christ and implores in true faith, finds saving cure of that incurable fountain of the passions . . . [which] fails and dries up through the power of Jesus only. Nothing else can cure this wound. . . . He came and took away the sin of the world. . . . And as that diseased woman spent all that she had upon those who professed to be able to cure her, but could be healed by none, until she approached the Lord, truly believing and touching the hem of his garment," so, he argues, nothing availed to cure the sickness of the human soul "until the Savior came, the true Physician, who cures mankind without cost, who gave himself as a ransom for mankind. He alone accomplished the great, saving deliverance and cure of the soul. He set it free from bondage, and brought it out of darkness, glorifying it with his own light" (homily 20). Of course, there needs to be a response, and Macarius is not slow to stress it. Referring both to the woman and to the blind man whom he had been using as another paradigm of salvation, he concludes, "Had not that blind man cried out, had not that sick woman come to the Lord, they would have found no cure. So unless a man comes to the Lord of his own free will, with wholehearted sincerity, and beseeches him with the assurance of faith, he finds no cure." It is moving to reflect that this kind of preaching was still to be found in the fourth century, which in many other ways had deviated significantly from the apostolic message. There can be no doubt that evangelism of this quality availed to bring countless thousands into the faith in the third and fourth centuries. Estimates from social scientists like Stark suggest that there may well have been some thirty million Christians by the year AD 350, about half of the population of the empire.

For Reflection

1. What were the strengths and weaknesses of monasteries?
2. How can the church best react in an age of nominal attachment?

3. What could be the modern equivalent of a couple of years spent in the desert before returning to public life?
4. There were great preachers in this period: what was their secret?

5

Celtic Evangelism

The towering figure in the early days of what we now call Celtic Christianity was undoubtedly Patrick (AD 389–461). Son of a Christian deacon in England, he was captured at the age of sixteen by Irish raiders and taken as a slave, probably to County Mayo. Though his people were Celts, he was also a Roman citizen, and his first language seems to have been Latin. During his years herding cattle as the slave of a Druid tribal chief, Patrick's teenage apathy about his traditional Christian faith changed. He began to pray a good deal and became a committed Christian. He developed a great sense of God in nature, and a growing understanding of the wild Irish people. He even came to love his captors. Only a word from on high in a dream, "You are going home," made him resolve to escape captivity and return to Britain. The next twenty-five years are obscure, but he spent some time in Gaul, probably at the monastery of Martin of Tours. Then at the age of forty-eight he heard in a dream the call "We beg you, holy servant, come and walk again among us." He was consecrated as the first bishop for the Irish and spent the rest of his life in the island. Thus began a ministry of startling originality and an impact that dominates Ireland to this day.

Although divided into many small tribes, with no towns or road system, this country of less than half a million people all spoke the same language and more or less shared the same culture. Because of his previous experience in the country, Patrick understood them. His approach was wise. He did not operate solo, for he had brought a team, with some priests and ordinands but mainly laypeople, with him from Gaul. First, he would contact the local chieftain or "king," having already gained the goodwill of High King Laoghaire. The team would make camp near one of their villages and engage in open-air speaking, praying for the sick and demonized, and employ visual symbols, poetry, and song. There would be much discussion in this preliterate, oral culture. The missionaries affirmed and built on every indigenous feature that they could, such as the native awareness of mystery, their sense of God's closeness, their belief in the afterlife, and their fascination with certain numbers, particularly the number three, which fed into the great emphasis Celtic Christianity gave to the Trinity. Thus the gospel was presented not as something entirely new, but as the fulfillment of all that was best in the indigenous culture. The team would spend weeks or months in the same area, and if there was response, would ask the local chief for a piece of land on which to build a simple wooden church. There are reports that over the years Patrick's mission planted some seven hundred churches! Once the church building was in place, Patrick would leave one of his priests behind to look after the people and move on. This team approach to evangelism was very attractive and very effective, and Patrick continued with it until his death.

Several features stand out. For one thing, the church was seen more as a flexible movement than an institution, which had increasingly become the pattern in Roman Christianity. It relied more on lay ministry than clergy. It was a lot closer to nature than the increasingly urban Christianity of much of Europe. It embraced the whole of life, not merely the spiritual side. And its emphasis was more on the immanence of God rather than his transcendence. Patrick embraced community living, which the best of the monastic tradition on the continent found so fruitful, but his communities were not so much an escape from the world as a launchpad for mission into the surrounding area. Celtic monasteries certainly included a few monks, but most were lay-people, farmers, craftsmen, and families. There was a threefold division of the day into worship, work, and study, but these were not isolated ascetic communities of the religious: they were largely a network of lay relationships, teeming with life, noise, and originality. This proved extremely attractive, and some of these "monasteries" attracted hundreds of adherents.

George Hunter in *The Celtic Way of Evangelism* draws several interesting contrasts between what he calls the Roman and Celtic ways of evangelism. Although he is mistaken in supposing that the "Roman" model neglected the barbarians, he is right in saying that the normal approach for evangelism in that day, as in evangelical circles today, was to present the Christian message, call on the hearers to respond, and then if they do, they are baptized and incorporated into the fellowship. The Celtic way was very different: first establish close relationship with people and make them at ease with your community, then within that fellowship engage them in conversation, discussion, prayer, and worship, and in time when they discover that they are drawn in by osmosis, you invite them to commit themselves to Christ in repentance, faith, and baptism. The first model, still very common in Western evangelism, starts with proclamation, aims for decision, and then draws new converts into fellowship. The Celtic model begins with fellowship, moves on to ministry and conversation, and leads to belief and an invitation to commitment. They were on to something important because, as John Finney showed in his research *Finding Faith Today*, for many people belonging comes before believing. Patrick was perhaps the first to make this important discovery.

Believers were nourished in these open monasteries, and in due course set out to bring the faith to other tribes. Mission teams setting out from these lively communities had a distinctive style. They traveled along the pathways of Irish culture with its love of song, poetry, imagination, and nature. Much evangelism then, as now, worked on the left brain, with logic, concepts, abstractions, language, and rational argument prominent. But many people today, as in ancient Ireland, respond better when their right brain is targeted: intuition, emotions, imagination, art, music, poetry, and experience. That was the route that Patrick pursued with such remarkable success.

The Druids had long been the traditional religious leaders in Ireland, but their power gradually decreased as the impact of the gospel grew. They relied much on secret magic, and it seems likely that the mystical, magical element so prominent in Celtic Christianity is a partial survival of pagan druidism, conquered by the greater power of Christ. The ancient hymn "St. Patrick's breastplate," which he may even have written himself, is a good example of this. "I bind unto myself today the strong name of the Trinity" suggests that the name of the Trinity is invoked as a very powerful charm that wards off evils of every sort. This is just one example of the way in which Patrick and his colleagues penetrated the minds of the Irish and presented the gospel in what we would call "cultural relevance," terms that they already understood.

Needless to say, countless legends gathered round this attractive, modest figure, but as Professor F. F. Bruce put it in *The Spreading Flame*, "Patrick's real greatness is impressive enough without such aids as these. It was he who brought within the orbit of imperial civilization and—better still—of Christian faith, a land that had never belonged to the empire politically. And he did so to such good purpose that when darkness fell over a great part of Western Europe, as it began to do even before his death, the true light continued to burn brightly in the island of saints and scholars and was carried forth from there to rekindle the lamps that had been extinguished."

Columba

The Celtic Christian movement continued to send missions into tribal areas, live alongside them, invite them to share in their community life, and thus grow new churches, which in turn sent out their own mission teams. In this way almost the whole of Ireland had become Christian within a century of Patrick's death. They then lifted up their eyes to wider horizons. In AD 563 a formidable leader, Columba, and a substantial team left Ireland for Iona, an island off the west coast of Scotland. This served as their base as they set about evangelizing the northern Picts, and re-evangelizing the southern Picts. Some of these had been reached earlier by Ninian, a leader in the Roman mold who lived in the late fourth and early fifth century, and set about reaching the partially Romanized Picts who lived just north of Hadrian's wall. According to Patrick, these had become "apostate" by his day. Interestingly, Bede tells us that Ninian was trained in Rome and set up his headquarters at Whitehorn, where he built a stone church, as the Romans would do—unlike the wooden or mud and wattle churches of the Irish Celts. Did these southern Picts fall away because the Christianity to which Ninian had introduced them was too Roman, too alien to their culture? At all events they were re-evangelized by the Irish Celts under Columba, whose approach was to go as far as possible with the flow of local culture, thus producing a truly indigenous church. And within a century most of Scotland had been won to Christ through the Celtic missions.

Aidan and Columbanus

Aidan was another intrepid Celtic pioneer. He set out from Iona to establish a monastic community on the tidal island of Lindisfarne, off the coast of northeast England. At this period in the early seventh century, England was being overwhelmed by hordes of Angles, Jutes, Saxons, and other continental peoples. Aidan and his companions, most of them Irish, set about cross-cultural mission. Following the example of Patrick and Columba, they multiplied these open monastic communities and used them to nourish and send out mission teams to repeat the process elsewhere. The work was difficult but, in the end, effective, and Aidan and his teams in the north of England probably made much more headway than Augustine in Kent where he had been sent as a missionary bishop by the pope in AD 597. He had brought with him a more conservative and Roman version of Christianity. Their method was to try to win the king and then filter down from there, the opposite of the Celtic mission strategy that was primarily directed to the common people.

Around the same time, c. AD 600, another Irish leader, Columbanus, and his team set out to reach continental Europe. They launched an amazing movement that reached France, Switzerland, Austria, Germany, and Italy. So through several generations of sustained indigenizing mission these Irish Celts went a long way toward the evangelization of Europe. One might imagine that this would please the British church, which had once commissioned Patrick to go to Ireland. But no. They repeatedly criticized the Celtic Christians for not adhering closely enough to Roman patterns. This came to a head in the Synod of Whitby in AD 664. Christian leaders loyal to Rome clashed with Celtic Christian leaders and upbraided them with two apparently superficial issues: the shape of their tonsures and the alternative date of Easter, which they celebrated using different calculations. The real reason, of course, was the unwillingness of the Catholic Christians to adapt to the indigenous methods of the Celts, and the determination to retain control. The Catholic Christians emphasized allegiance to Rome, Latin as the language of worship, and the imposition of Roman cultural ways on those who professed the faith. Their victory spelled the end of Celtic Christianity. They had no central organization that could match that of Rome. They had, perforce, to submit or be banished, and Roman Christianity took over. This was a tragedy, for it squashed the free-flowing initiative, imagination, and cultural sensitivity of the Celtic Christians, and it led to the Roman-type monasteries that did very little to evangelize the local population, and by the Middle Ages these had often fallen prey to the mismanagement, greed, and immorality that evoked the protest of the Reformation.

Strengths of Celtic Christianity

We cannot fail to be impressed with many aspects of Celtic Christianity. They were not afraid to try something for the first time. Their approach was relaxed and flexible. They worked as a team. They combined the nurture of the monastery with perpetual outreach in mission. They believed in the power of outreach by mission teams. They were strong on the need to understand the culture and interpret the gospel so that ordinary people could understand it. They had a love for the common man. They had a great respect for nature, and their evangelism concerned the whole person, not merely the spiritual side, embracing creation as well as redemption. They used visual, artistic symbols such as the famous Celtic knot and Celtic cross. They knew the evangelistic impact of community rather than individual ministry. They had a sustained passion to reach out, often with most inadequate resources. This characteristic stands in sharp contrast to almost all denominations then as now where leadership is institutional rather than missional. They did not buy into the generally accepted view in the Roman empire that tribes need to be somewhat civilized before they can be effectively evangelized. Instead, they took pains to understand the mindset of the barbarians to whom they went and to reach them in a way they understood and valued. They did not try to impose their Christianity from above but allowed people to see the authenticity of their lives, explore their spirituality, and in due course share it.

George Hunter in *The Celtic Way of Evangelism* has pointed out many ways in which our postmodern culture is analogous to the barbarian culture of ancient Ireland. He shrewdly observes, "The typical church ignores two populations, year after year: the people who are not 'refined' enough to feel comfortable with us, and the people who are too 'out of control' for us to be comfortable with them." And he points out the many ways in which some communities in North America where he lives are forsaking traditional church models and learning from the warm, intuitive, culturally relevant paths trodden by those Celtic saints of long ago. The Celts certainly have much to teach us.

For Reflection

1. Does my proclamation of the gospel appeal only to the left brain of my hearers?
2. How far do I go in seeking to understand the culture of my hearers before preaching to them?
3. Does the gospel I preach look more like an authoritative doctrinal message from above or the fulfillment of the best ideals and aspirations of the hearers?
4. Do I have anything in my church to correspond to the warm, open, nourishing community of these early monasteries, and to the mission teams that regularly emerged from them?
5. How can I learn to sustain evangelism as these Celts did over long periods?
6. Is my gospel seen to affect the whole of life or just the spiritual area?

6

Lights in the Darkness

Rightly called the "Dark Ages," the medieval period was not celebrated for evangelism. Outreach from the Roman Catholic Church, as it had become, consisted in either persuading or forcing people to get baptized, for baptism was seen as the gateway into the church, and the church alone could convey salvation. Worship was very formal and often mumbled by priests who could hardly read to congregations that could not understand. The central act of worship was the mass, in which Christ was offered afresh under the guise of bread and wine for the sins of the world. The Bible did not figure much: it was only available in Latin, a language few ordinary people knew, though they recognized some stories from the Gospels because they were illustrated in stained glass. The relics of the saints were greatly revered, almost as magic charms. Heaven and hell were prominent in the teaching of the church, along with purgatory where, after death, the evil in the lives of Christians was painfully purged away: but if you could afford to pay for masses to be offered for your soul, you could minimize your time in purgatory. Indulgences were sold, which were also supposed to relieve you from your time in purgatory. During these centuries, the church became increasingly corrupt. The pope exercised temporal as well as spiritual power. He kept an army and held absolute power in the church. Some of the popes lived openly with their mistresses and sired illegitimate children, a practice that was not lost on the priests who, though vowed to celibacy, often cohabited with nuns or local women. Clergy vied for leading positions in the church, which were sometimes sold to the highest bidder, and the monasteries were often cesspits of immorality. Dark days indeed.

Nevertheless, there were glorious examples of those who stood out against the corruption of the church, espoused the lifestyle of the New Testament, and courageously evangelized. Let us glance at three of them, hailing from different countries. They have much to teach us about seeking to proclaim and live the gospel in the midst of a church that has radically departed from scriptural norms.

Peter Waldo

The first of these was Peter Waldo. We do not know as much as we would like about his life. But he was apparently a wealthy merchant, living in Lyons in southern France, until he had a profound encounter with Christ in around AD 1170. This led him to regard possessions as a major hindrance to preaching the gospel. He was deeply impressed by the words of Jesus to a rich man like himself, "If you want to be perfect, go, sell your possessions and give to the poor, and you will have treasure in heaven. Then come, follow me" (Matthew 19:21). He took this literally and after making financial provision for his wife and children, Waldo gave the rest of his possessions to the poor. Needless to say, this made a big impact, and as Peter Waldo went preaching the gospel through the towns and villages of southern France, others joined him, made the same sacrifices, and became known as the Poor Men of Lyons. At first the church looked favorably on this surprising phenomenon, and Waldo was welcomed by the pope and allowed to preach so long as he secured the goodwill of local priests and bishops first. This was not a condition Waldo was disposed to obey. He and his Poor Men continued their attractive preaching to the poor everywhere, but the contrast between the biblical simplicity of their lifestyle and the luxury in which the leaders of the church lived was too stark to be endured. Accordingly, they were excommunicated at the Council of Verona in 1184. Persecution followed, savage in some places, and it continued for centuries. Only in 2015 did the pope apologize to the Waldensians for the terrible treatment meted out to them by the Roman Catholic Church

It is not surprising that they made such an impact. Most of them were laymen and they preached in the language of the people, not Latin. They expounded the Scriptures, which would have been largely unknown in those days. Indeed, Waldo is credited with being the first European to try to produce a translation of the Bible into the common tongue. He and his followers committed large tracts of Scripture to memory, which gave added impact to their preaching. They took great pains to reach the poor whom the Catholic Church of the day neglected. They embraced voluntary poverty and lived, like their near contemporary Francis of Assisi (1181–1226), on the hospitality of their hearers. Their lives, like his, were even more powerful than their words.

The teachings of Waldo and his followers are noteworthy. On the positive side, they affirmed the centrality of Scripture, the fall of mankind, the complete atonement achieved by Jesus, and the need for faith in him. They exalted the value of poverty and they stressed the importance of preaching the gospel by men and women alike. On the negative side, they protested against relics of the saints, which they denounced as bogus; holy water, which they deemed no better than any other water; masses for the living and the dead; and pilgrimages and other attempts to gain merit with God, and they were clear that prayer in a barn was just as valid as prayer in a church building. In due course they were so shocked by the corruption of the Catholic Church that they called her the harlot of the Apocalypse.

The motto of Peter Waldo was *"Lux lucet in tenebris"* ("light glows in the darkness") and it was very apt. They did shine brightly in the spiritual darkness around them. They lived very simply. They preached the Bible, particularly the Sermon on the Mount. They proclaimed good news to all who would listen. They concentrated on the poor and marginalized and brought them the message of the gospel in the language people understood. Not surprisingly, they influenced later reforming groups, and they were in many ways precursors of the Reformation.

John Wycliffe

More than 150 years later, John Wycliffe (1329–1384) trod a somewhat similar path. A quiet and distinguished Oxford don, the Master of Balliol, he was a noted theologian and philosopher and attracted little attention until the last decade of his life, when he threw himself into the cause of reform. Probably the change was triggered by his visit to the pope in Avignon in 1373, where he was greatly shocked by the luxury and corruption he observed. At all events, from this time he started sending out evangelists. These Poor Priests, as he called them, commonly known as Lollards, were itinerant preachers who lived with great simplicity. Wearing long brown robes and sandals, they carried a staff but no purse, living as they did on the generosity of their hearers. They preached in English, not ecclesiastical Latin, and did not ask for money. Their message was biblical, and they relied considerably on the teaching Wycliffe had given them while studying under him at Oxford. These young evangelists were initially priests, but later on Wycliffe sent out laymen and laywomen as well, contending that God's call was more important than man's ordination. He did not set out to be a rebel or to establish a new order of mobile ministers. He just wanted ordinary people to hear the gospel in their own language, preached with simplicity and force by messengers of integrity who had clearly sacrificed much to fulfill their vocation. Wycliffe was convinced of the authority and power of the Bible and undertook a translation of it into the vernacular that still survives today. This was the main weapon in the hands of the Lollards whose job it was to expound the text of Scripture and make it plain. The Lollards won a lot of popularity: many joined them, and they went everywhere throughout the villages and small towns of England.

In due course, this angered the Roman Catholic Church, particularly as Wycliffe found himself in contention with several of their dearly held positions. Censured by the pope in 1377, he wrote a book in 1378 entitled *On the Truth of Holy Scripture*, maintaining that the Bible was the supreme authority for Christians, the measure of orthodox teaching, and the guide for reform of church and individual believer. It was quite sufficient by itself to lead a person to salvation. This was in direct opposition to the Roman Catholic assertion that salvation was only possible through the church. Moreover, he believed that anyone could understand the main thrust of Scripture if they had faith in Christ and relied on the guidance of the Holy Spirit. They did not need priests, who were often very ignorant, to interpret the Bible to them. Wycliffe's strong conviction about the authority and sufficiency of Scripture led him to question the sale of indulgences, prayers to the saints, the very existence of monasteries, and the doctrine of transubstantiation. His reliance on Scripture also led him to reject the authority of the pope (especially as there were two rival popes in his day), and he was clear that Christ alone was the head of the church. He was the first to express the belief in the "invisible church," that is to say that the true church consisted in those God had predestined to salvation, rather than those formally enrolled in the Catholic Church.

The Catholic hierarchy managed to evict him from his position in Oxford, and he retired to Lutterworth, where he devoted himself to writing tracts for his Poor Priests to take with them and to supervising and sharing in the translation of the Bible from the Latin Vulgate. He died peacefully in 1384, escaping the martyrdom that other reformers had to endure, since he had friends in high places. The Roman Church did not burn him alive: they simply dug up and burned his bones!

Wycliffe is rightly known as the Morning Star of the Reformation. His emphasis on the Bible as the norm of Christian faith and life, his fearless stand against corruption, his passion for evangelism, his denunciation of false teaching, and his belief, though not quite expressed in those terms, in the priesthood of all believers led directly to the central convictions of the Reformers a century later. Perhaps his greatest achievement was instilling into his Poor Priests the assurance that the Bible contains all that is necessary for salvation. Hence their determination to pass on its message despite the opposition and persecution that came their way. It remains the case today that strong biblical preaching is one of the most effective methods of evangelism.

Jan Hus

A third example of light shining in the darkness was Jan Hus, a near contemporary and admirer of Wycliffe. His home country was Bohemia, the modern Czech Republic. He was a priest and professor at the prestigious University of Prague, and he then became its rector. In 1402 he became the main preacher at the Bethlehem Chapel in Prague, a building that held some three thousand people standing up! This was regularly packed with people of all sorts, particularly peasants, but he appealed to the aristocracy as well and was confessor to the queen, who would often visit the Bethlehem Chapel. Hus made a point of preaching in the Czech language, thus breaking the German monopoly over the Bohemian Church of his day. This regular preaching work drove Hus to a deeper study of the Scriptures. Like Wycliffe, he became convinced of the authority of the Bible, both for doctrine and for daily living. He made preaching from the Bible the main feature in the worship of the chapel. He found himself in agreement with most of Wycliffe's teaching and, like him, sought to eliminate corruption in the church and encourage scriptural simplicity. Ordered to surrender all the writings of Wycliffe for burning, he refused. This infuriated the German faction in the university, who complained to the bishop of Prague, who was also a German. Consequently, Hus was excommunicated in 1410 and forced to leave his post in the university. He retired to the hills where he continued to write and to preach in the countryside. He was summoned in 1414 to the Council of Constance and required to explain his views. When he arrived, fearing for his safety, he discovered that his fears were fully justified. He was betrayed, arrested, and although there was a trial of sorts he was not allowed to defend himself. He endured a miserable period of imprisonment and eventually was burned at the stake in 1415, singing a hymn of praise to Christ. His death led to extensive riots, and the pope sent an army to crush them. From the survivors of that war emerged the Bohemian Brethren, who eventually emigrated to Germany and evolved into the Moravians.

Three different men in three different countries. They were all beacons of light in a dark period of the church's life. They had a lot in common.

Qualities These Men Had in Common

None of them originally wanted to secede from the Catholic Church. They wanted to reform it, and it was the refusal of the authorities to listen to their claims, backed though they were by the Scriptures that the church professed to believe, that drove them or their followers into separation.

All of them came to have an overwhelming respect for the inspiration and authority of Holy Scripture. They wanted to make it the guide for their lives, their teaching, and the whole church.

All of them were driven by their study of Scripture to expose the corruption in the church, false teachings like transubstantiation, indulgences, purgatory, and the temporal and spiritual power of the pope. These things were all deeply ingrained in the church and yet found no support in the church's foundation documents, the Scriptures.

All of them had a great concern for the common people, steeped as they were in ignorance, since nobody taught them or seemed to care for them. The compassion of Christ welled up in these men and they made the common people, especially the poor, their main concern.

As a result of this concern, all three of them energetically engaged in preaching the gospel to the poor, although to do so was to incur the opposition of the rich and influential. That is why ordinary people loved them, followed them, and clamored to hear them.

All these men were filled with courage and were prepared to put their lives on the line for the truth of what they proclaimed.

All of them realized the importance of working with a team and leaving a legacy of followers who would continue the work and indeed eclipse their founders. Waldo's work led to the influential Waldensian Church, Wycliffe's to the Lollards, and Hus's followers, the Hussites, represented the first successful challenge to the authoritarian claims of the Roman Catholic Church. Truly these men represented *lux in tenebris*, light in the darkness.

For Reflection

1. How prepared am I to face opposition and even persecution for my beliefs?
2. Do I in fact make the teachings of the Bible my guide in all matters of faith and conduct?
3. Do I care enough for the poor, disadvantaged, and hostile to bend my energies to reach them?
4. Am I prepared to stand up against the wrong things in the church that compromise the gospel—even if they are widely accepted?
5. Am I investing in the next generation who can carry on the work?

7

The Reformation

In the fifteenth and sixteenth centuries, both church and state throughout Europe were going through a period of great upheaval, dramatic change, and deep division. Men were crying out for reform. Civil unrest plagued the German states, where the Reformation began. Successive years of crop failure brought near despair. The feudal system was beginning to give way to the emergence of work in the towns. The invention of the printing press changed the intellectual situation dramatically as a growing proportion of the population became literate and was able to enjoy the intellectual fruits of the Renaissance. Erasmus's recently published Greek New Testament was immensely influential in leading many to start studying the New Testament in depth. Meanwhile, the church remained under the pope, still selling indulgences, worshipping images, selling positions of leadership, and the other failings that had been exposed and denounced in the previous century. It was like a parched field, dry as tinder, and Luther's famous nailing of his ninety-five theses to the church door was the spark that turned it into a conflagration that embraced the whole of Northern Europe and still has massive social, economic, and religious implications today. It is obviously impossible to trace the various aspects of this mighty revolution here, but evangelism is our subject and so I propose to take a number of the key figures of the Reformation and see what they contributed to the re-evangelism of Europe.

Martin Luther

Martin Luther (1483–1546) was born to a father who was trying to make a living through mining in the German town of Eisleben. Martin showed promise as a lad, went to the University of Erfurt, and was on his way to a career in law when he was caught in a violent storm and nearly killed by a thunderbolt that knocked him off his feet. He viewed God as a fearsome judge and promised that if his life was spared he would become a monk. He kept his promise, and, to his father's displeasure, joined the Augustinian order, thus exchanging his carefree student life for one of severe mortification and self-denial. Life in a monastery was tough, with little food and more than six hours a day in chapel. But Luther adapted because he wanted to appease this God of judgment and save his soul. He became morbidly scrupulous about his sins and spent hours in the confessional. He was ordained priest, and in due course he became a professor of biblical studies at the new University of Wittenberg, a post he retained until his death. In 1517 he reflected on the sale of indulgences, designed to fast-track the soul's path through purgatory. He was scandalized by Johann Tetzel, an indulgence-monger who advertised his sales with the jingle, "When the coin in the coffer rings, the soul from purgatory springs"—without any need for repentance or confession.

So, on All Saints Day 1517, Luther nailed his ninety-five theses about indulgences to the door of the Castle Church. His aim was not to start a revolution but to initiate a debate. However, to argue theology was one thing: to deprive a cash-strapped papacy trying to rebuild St. Peter's of much-needed income was another. Overnight Luther found himself at the heart of a storm. He became instantly well known. Crowds flocked to hear him preach. His ninety-five theses were all over Germany in two weeks, and all over Europe in a month— such was the power of the printing press and the enthusiasm of his followers. Tetzel called for him to be burned as a heretic, and within four years he was excommunicated by the pope after refusing to recant his writings. But he still had to face the emperor, Charles V. This took place at the Diet of Worms in 1521. When challenged to recant his written opinions, Luther gave his famous reply. "I am bound by the Scripture I have quoted and my conscience is captive to the word of God. I cannot and will not recant anything I have written. Here I stand. I can do no other. So help me God." He was then outlawed. The church would gladly have burned him at the stake, but Prince Frederick of Saxony protected him, and he went into hiding in Wartburg Castle, where he translated first the New Testament and then the Old into German. His translation became the standard for German prose for many years. However, his aim was not literary excellence but evangelistic impact. He wanted to put God's word in the hands of the ordinary people.

For there had been a radical change in this erstwhile monk's theology. He had been brought up to see God as the fierce judge ("I did not love, yes, I hated the righteous God who punishes sinners"). But as he prepared his lectures on Romans, he made a life-changing discovery. It lay in Romans 1:17, "The righteous will live by faith." "I began to understand that the righteousness of God is that by which the righteous lives by a gift of God, namely by faith. . . . Here I felt that I was altogether born again and had entered paradise itself through open gates."

This was the central discovery of the Reformation: but not a new truth, simply the new understanding of what the Scriptures had always taught. In due course it changed the face of Europe. But with this new understanding of justification (being put right with God, by his grace alone and through faith alone to the glory of God alone), went Luther's new understanding of the ground on which God could do this. God condemns before he saves. But Christ bore our condemnation once and for all before he was raised to new life. So, the believer needs to come with empty hands, stripped of all self-righteousness, all attempts to gain merit, to receive with deep gratitude the status of "justified" won for him by the death of Christ. Luther came to see that the deep despair over his spiritual state which he had long felt did not disqualify him from God's grace: it was in fact the only qualification for it.

This was revolutionary indeed. And before long it led to the launch of the Lutheran Church, which spread all over Northern Europe. It led countless thousands to the new birth that Luther himself had discovered. And it led to a massive transformation of life and morals, as he taught his students: "We are not made righteous by doing righteous works; but rather we do righteous works by being made righteous." Luther continued to preach each week and to teach in the university after his excommunication. His clear exposition of Scripture gripped his students, many of whom came from abroad and returned to their homes to spread the message all over Europe.

This is not the place to look at his social and political achievements, but Luther's achievements in the field of evangelism were very significant.

First, he rediscovered the truth, so dear to St. Paul and St. Augustine, that we are put right with God not by our (painfully inadequate) good deeds, not by ruthless monastic discipline and self-mortification, but by faith in God's loving welcome, guaranteed by Christ's death on the cross and received in adoring faith. That is the message that produces new men and women. And Luther certainly lived to see it on a massive scale.

Second, his translation of the Bible into the language of the people enabled the truths he had found there to spread far and wide. In addition, his own writings to explain and commend the gospel were extensive. His many pamphlets and other publications achieved great influence in educated circles throughout Europe, not least Britain.

Third, Luther's conviction of the authority and inspiration of the Bible, over against the corrupt teaching and lifestyle of the church hierarchy, was of decisive significance. He restored it to its proper place in worship and evangelism. Whenever there was a question over church teaching or the Bible's teaching, there was only one answer!

Fourth, he was clear on the priesthood of all believers, and this not only gave new confidence to the laity but enabled them confidently to pass on to others the gospel that had changed their lives.

Finally, Luther was a competent musician, and he knew the power of music in worship. So he wrote a number of hymns, most important of which was *Eine feste Burg ist unser Gott*, "A Mighty Fortress Is Our God," and encouraged congregational singing in his churches.

This man's life was not a perfect model of sainthood: far from it. He was militant, anti-Semitic, and coarse. But his sheer courage in the face of ecclesiastical and political opposition is a great example to evangelists, who, if they are faithful to Scripture, often have to take a lonely and principled stand. Supremely, Luther's life shows how God can take a humble, ordinary man, with all his failings, and make him the channel of blessing to millions. That exhibits grace alone, and it redounds to the glory of God alone.

John Calvin

The spark that Luther had ignited turned rapidly into a forest fire. Ulrich Zwingli (1484–1531), a contemporary of Luther, became a celebrated preacher of the gospel. He was called to the cathedral at Zurich to be "the people's priest," and he demonstrated it at once by preaching in German, the language of the people, rather than Latin as was expected. In addition to preaching, he engaged in public debate, at which he was very skillful, and the city was won over to the cause of reform. His life was cut short by death in a battle against Catholic forces in 1531. The Anabaptists ("Rebaptizers") originally emerged from the followers of Zwingli in Zurich. They were the radical wing of the Reformation and wanted to abolish any practice not explicitly taught in Scripture, while insisting on believers' baptism rather than infant baptism as practiced by most Reformers, including Luther and Zwingli. But they were important, despite being divided and having no central leadership. For one thing, they launched the great Baptist tradition in the subsequent church. But even more important, they were such avid evangelists. Perhaps we need to remember that God greatly blessed the evangelistic ministry of men who differed on important doctrinal issues: passion for Jesus is more important than doctrinal correctness.

But unquestionably the greatest of the Reformers after Luther was John Calvin (1509–1564), who was twenty-six years his junior. He was a Frenchman, but he had to leave Paris after his radical encounter with Christ in 1533. He went to live in Basel. Amazingly, it was only three years later that he published the first version of his great doctrinal work *Institutes of the Christian Religion,* which turned out to be the most influential of all the books in the Reformation. He saw Adam's sin as rebellion against God by which all men and women are corrupted. They deserve God's judgment and can do nothing to merit salvation, but God comes to the rescue. Though he hates sin, he loves the sinner so much that he sent his Son to die in our place. Jesus satisfied the righteous judgment of God, reversed the curse of Adam's sin, and destroyed spiritual death for those who are linked to Christ by repentance and faith. Calvin was clear that the true church consisted not of everyone who was baptized irrespective of their faith but of those who God foreknew would turn to him. One might imagine that this strong emphasis on election would make Calvin indifferent to evangelism. Some subsequent Calvinists have certainly made that mistake: if God has chosen those he will save, why should we bother to do anything about it? But in this respect the followers were very different from their leader. Calvin himself was a passionate evangelist, as we shall see. Dr. Lindsay Brown has helped me to see the extent of his evangelistic work, and I am much indebted to him.

In 1536 Calvin visited Geneva and stayed there for much of the rest of his life. His evangelism revolutionized the city, and Protestant refugees from all over Europe flooded into it because it was run as a model Christian state. It is fascinating today to see in the old quarter of the town how many houses had been extended by a further story to accommodate the influx. The gospel dominated the city, and it became known throughout Europe as the center of evangelism and a living laboratory for Christian social life.

As for his evangelistic passion, Calvin loved Matthew 28:19, the Great Commission, and commented, "The Lord orders the ministers of the gospel to go far out to scatter the teaching of salvation throughout all the regions of the earth." In commenting on Acts 2, he wrote, "The Spirit comes for the gospel to reach all the ends and extremes of the world." On Isaiah 12 he comments that Isaiah "shows that it is our duty to proclaim the goodness of God to every nation. While we exhort and encourage others, we must not at the same time sit down in indolence: but it is proper that we set an example before others, for nothing can be more absurd than to see lazy and slothful men who are exciting others to praise God."

He writes much about the kingdom of God, and he is clear that its extension is primarily God's work. But men have a vital part in it, too. This is essentially fourfold. First, he insists on prayer for those who do not know Christ: "God bids us to pray for the salvation of unbelievers," he wrote, and this emphasis on prayer for the lost comes out strongly in the liturgy he compiled for the church in Geneva. Second, he is clear that we are all called to commend the gospel both by our words and by our deeds. He set up an academy in Geneva where, in addition to children, he trained ministers and evangelists. Many came from other countries, and they returned home with the passion for evangelism in their hearts and the *Institutes* in their hands. His third avenue for reaching others was through godly rulers, who can have great influence; the impact of the queen of Navarre was a case in point. But a further way of evangelism that he valued highly was the printed word. The Geneva Bible, produced under his aegis, soon became dominant. In England it largely replaced Henry VIII's Great Bible through the verve and freshness of its translation. It antedated the King James Version by more than fifty years and was the Bible of Shakespeare, Donne, Bunyan, and most of the English church. It was carried to America in the *Mayflower*! There were thirty-four printing houses in Geneva by the time of Calvin's death, and he made good use of them. His commentaries on the New Testament were lucid and pungent. They went all over Europe and are still invaluable today. He encouraged missionary work in Spain, Poland, Hungary, Britain, and the Netherlands. But most of all he made great efforts to reach his native France, and between 1555 and 1562 he and his colleagues sent no less than eighty-eight missionaries there. This mission was so effective that within four years he had more than two thousand congregations in France, and the Huguenots (French Calvinists) numbered around two million. It is high time that this myth about Calvin's disinterest in evangelism is laid to rest. He wrote, "If we have any humanity in us, seeing men going to perdition, ought we not to be moved with pity to rescue the poor souls from hell and teach them the way of salvation?" It is clear that his practice matched his words. He even sent a missionary to Brazil. So, despite his heavy involvement in the running of the city, and despite his academic training in the academy, evangelism remained a top priority for this remarkable man.

Calvin did not have the personal warmth and cheerfulness of Luther. He was reserved and neither courted nor gained much popularity. He was often at odds with the secular authorities in Geneva. Yet people were deeply attracted by the clarity of his teaching, his emphasis on Scripture, and the organization and discipline of the Christian community in Geneva. By the time of his death, he had set in place the best organized and longest lasting expression of the Reformation in continental Europe. His missionary work was extremely effective, particularly in his own country, France. His training in the academy had an enormous impact, and one of his associates was John Knox, who returned to be the fearless evangelist of Scotland.

The Reformation in England

In Germany the start of the Reformation was noble. In Switzerland it was well taught and well organized. But in England it was neither of these things. It was, initially at least, largely political. Henry's desire to be rid of his prematurely aging queen, Catherine, in order to marry Anne Boleyn is well known. It led to Henry's rejecting the pope and assuming the rule of head of the English church himself. (This was not altogether unprecedented. The princes in North Germany had also disposed of the pope as just another bishop with no rightful power in their realms.) Henry plucked Thomas Cranmer from obscurity to become archbishop of Canterbury, and he stayed loyal to Henry through thick and thin. This landed him in some very compromising positions, including the declaration of the royal supremacy and in due course the execution of Anne Boleyn. Cranmer was not a courageous man, but he had been influenced by the new learning, partly the humanism of Erasmus and then the work of Luther. He became increasingly drawn toward the position of the Reformers, as did several of the nobility in England and at least two of Henry's own queens.

William Tyndale (1494–1536) was another of the heroic Reformation evangelists. Cranmer was deeply impressed by Tyndale's translation of the Bible from the original Hebrew and Greek (unlike Wycliffe's translation from the Latin Vulgate). Whereas anyone found owning a copy of Wycliffe's Bible could be condemned to death, the invention of Caxton's printing press opened the flood gates, and Tyndale's translation was soon in massive demand. England became too dangerous for him, and he set up shop on the continent, whence large quantities of English Bibles got smuggled into England in the 1520s. When charged with heresy before the ignorant chancellor of Gloucester, he had boldly declared, "If God spare my life, ere many years I will cause the boy that drives the plough to know more of the Scriptures than you." He was as good as his word, and the Bible in English became widely read in the country. In 1536 he was betrayed, arrested, and strangled at the stake before his body was burned. His final words were, "Lord, open the king of England's eyes." That prayer was answered because three years later, largely through the good offices of Cranmer, the king authorized the Great Bible, ironically largely based on Tyndale's translation, to be set up in every church so that the people could read it for themselves. This was something hitherto unheard of. It was immensely popular, and a second edition had to be produced a year later, to which Archbishop Cranmer, who was leaning more and more toward the views of the continental Reformers Luther and Calvin, wrote a commendatory foreword.

Multiple Changes

On the whole, it seems ordinary Englishmen did not bother a great deal about the removal of the pope's authority, although Thomas More was prepared to die for it. They remembered the greed and arrogance of Cardinal Thomas Wolsey, the pope's legate in England, though they were probably angered by the suppression of the monasteries, their treasures ransacked and their lands acquired by the crown. But when Henry died and Edward VI came to the throne for a few short years, it was a different story. Cranmer, who had long been a quiet friend of reform, produced the 1549 Prayer Book, speedily followed by a more Protestant version in 1552. You can imagine the confusion this caused in the minds of parishioners, most of whom did not understand what the theological debates were all about but missed the familiar church adornments and the Latin mass. When Edward died in 1553, England was by no means a Protestant country, despite the energetic evangelistic preaching of bishops like Hugh Latimer, Nicholas Ridley, and increasingly Thomas Cranmer. What really turned the tide in England was the burning of Protestant leaders by the passionately Catholic Queen Mary. Within eighteen months, she had ensured the burning alive of some three hundred Protestant sympathizers, including the bishops of London and Worcester and the archbishop, Cranmer, himself. She may have thought that their Protestant faith was shallow and that they would easily recant and resume allegiance to the pope. If so, she was very wrong. The sheer courage of these martyrs made an enormous impression on people. As the Reformation historian Owen Chadwick put it, "The steadfastness of the victims, from Ridley and Latimer downwards, baptized the English Reformation in blood and drove into English minds the fatal association of ecclesiastical tyranny with the See of Rome." Ten years earlier the Protestant cause had been identified in the public mind with desecration of churches, suppression of monasteries, destruction of images, and religious anarchy, but now people began to associate the Reformed faith with courage, honesty, and loyal English opposition to government that leaned toward the old enemy, Spain, rather than the interests of the British people.

Martyrs and Evangelists

The manner of these men's deaths was indeed amazing. Thomas Bilney, a Cambridge academic, was the first to die, in 1531, at the instigation of Wolsey. Bilney had led Hugh Latimer to Christ, and he was still a young man of thirty-one. People were weeping as he was chained to the stake, but seeing those who had brought about his condemnation, he freely forgave them, and he died crying "Jesus, Credo!" In 1555 Latimer and Ridley, both bishops, were chained back-to-back at the stake outside Balliol College, Oxford. And Latimer, famous preacher that he was, gave his shortest and most celebrated address: "Be of good comfort, Master Ridley, and play the man. We shall this day light such a candle by God's grace in England as I trust shall never be put out." Latimer died quickly, but Ridley suffered terribly. Yet that candle has never been put out. It was reignited by the death of Thomas Cranmer. The archbishop did not die with Ridley and Latimer. Through fear of the stake, he recanted his Protestant views and signed up to Catholic doctrine. But the queen wanted him dead all the same, and he was rearrested and after two and a half years in prison was executed in 1556. He regained his courage when the test came. Abandoning the prepared Latin recantation, he cried, "Forasmuch as my hand offended in writing contrary to my heart, therefore my hand shall be punished first." True to his word, he thrust his hand into the heart of the fire. It was by this famous gesture that he proclaimed his true faith and triumphed by the manner of his death. Queen

Mary was determined to kill these great Protestant leaders, hoping that this would squash the movement. But her plan backfired. Sympathy for the martyrs swept the country. It was Mary the Catholic who made England Protestant.

But these Reformers were not simply courageous martyrs for their faith. They were avid preachers of the gospel. They lived dangerously under Henry VIII when a single word that offended the king could cost you your head. But with the accession of his Protestant son Edward, everything changed for a brief six years—before Mary came to the throne. Cranmer had abolished the countless different Latin rites held in different parts of the country, and in 1549 published a single Prayer Book in English to be used in every church. It was influenced by Luther and was well on the way to classical Reformation teaching. But in fact, the book satisfied nobody. The conservatives saw it as too radical and the reformers saw it as too conservative. So, in 1552 Cranmer brought out a Prayer Book strongly revised in a Reformed direction. Statues were smashed or removed from churches, wall paintings whitewashed over, worship of the saints abolished, every trace of transubstantiation expunged, the altar replaced by a Communion table, vestments abolished, and prayers for the dead discontinued. He issued a Book of Homilies so that incompetent priests who could not preach effectively could read them to their congregations. In addition, a Bible in English was installed in every church. This was a massive outreach to the people of this country. But it lasted only a year. When Mary came to the throne, the Prayer Book was banished, the Bibles removed, the mass and papal supremacy restored. And then the burnings began.

So, although no great evangelist himself, Cranmer used his position as archbishop to make generous provision for the whole country to read the gospel in the Scriptures and have a Prayer Book that was biblically sound and accessible to everyone in their own language. A massive achievement.

Meanwhile, many others became distinguished preachers. Among them nobody surpassed Hugh Latimer, known as the poor man's friend and as the apostle of England. He had an astonishingly powerful preaching ministry not only to the king and courtiers but to the humblest peasants. Nicholas Ridley, when he became bishop of London, visited all the clergy, an almost unheard-of innovation, and checked that they were carrying out the new services. He was a celebrated preacher and could be seen in St. Paul's preaching in the forenoon and in the afternoon at the cross until almost five o'clock so that the mayor and others had to go home by torchlight! He had a great concern for the poor and once, when preaching before the king, he spoke movingly about the need for practical charity. Edward was deeply touched and made grants of lands, houses, and revenues, which led to the foundation of Christ's Hospital and gave Bridewell, "the ancient mansion of many English kings," as an orphanage.

Another great reformer and evangelist was John Hooper, made bishop of Gloucester in 1551. Foxe says this of him in his *Book of Martyrs*: "So careful was he in his cure that he left neither pains untaken nor ways unsought how to train up the flock of Christ in the true Word of salvation, continually labouring in the same." He led his diocese "as though he had in charge but one family. No father of his household, no gardener in his garden, no husbandman in his vineyard was more or better occupied than he in his diocese among his flock, going about his towns and villages teaching and preaching to the people there." He was only in the post for a couple of years, and when Mary came to the throne, he was deposed and cast into the notorious Fleet prison for eighteen months before being burned alive. One nobleman urged him to recant and save his life, saying, "Life is sweet and death is bitter." To which Hooper returned the memorable answer, "The life to come is more sweet and the death to come is more bitter." Such was the profound conviction and immense courage of these heroic leaders of the English Reformation. They proclaimed the gospel by their preaching and lifestyle, and they commended it by the way they died.

Achievements of the Reformers

When we reflect on the key elements in the immense impact made by the reformers in Europe, a number of things stand out.

First, they were insistent that the authority of the Bible was more important than any pope or church council. So they saw that it was translated into the language of the people and made widely available.

Second, they made excellent use of the latest technology, the printing press. It made the rapid dissemination of their writings, as well as the Bible itself, readily available.

Third, the great New Testament doctrine of justification by God's grace, received in faith, to the glory of God alone was rescued from the obscurity into which it had fallen under the medieval church. The preaching of God's grace brought new life, new self-confidence to rich and poor alike, and it led to a new lifestyle out of gratitude to God.

Fourth, the pope's absolute control of the church, nowhere justified in Scripture, was broken.

Fifth, the biblical awareness of the priesthood of all believers, and their ability to go to God without the intervention of a priest, transformed the religion of Europe.

Finally, the reformers discovered that much of Europe was ripe for change, and they took full advantage of the social and political circumstances. No evangelists operate in a vacuum. Context is important. It is noteworthy that the context in Northern Europe favored reform and it flourished, while in the south of the continent, Spain and Italy, it did not.

For Reflection

1. Does my evangelism and that of my church reflect the balance of biblical teaching, or does it rely on one particular approach, or proof texts?
2. Do we make full use of the web and the opportunities of the digital age?
3. Are we so convinced of the truth of the gospel that we are prepared to withstand opposition and, if need be, die for it?
4. Are we prepared to proclaim biblical truth even when the church is mired in political correctness?
5. If I am not an evangelist myself, do I use my influence, as Cranmer did, to provide opportunities for those who are?
6. What are the opportunities in our culture to break through with the gospel?

8

The Evangelical Revival

This is one of the most impressive examples of widespread evangelism anywhere in the world. It took place in England in the eighteenth century, largely through the ministry of the Wesley brothers and George Whitefield. So let us set the scene.

Eighteenth-Century Society and Religion

The new spiritual life engendered by the Reformation had died, and the prospects both in society and in the church looked about as bad as could be. Britain was proverbial for drunkenness, as much among the nobility as the ordinary people. The squires boasted of being "six bottle men"—who nowadays could drink six bottles of port at a sitting? Gin was sold from barrows in the streets with the famous sign, "Drunk for a penny, dead drunk for twopence, clean straw for nothing." There was gross immorality everywhere: the prince of Wales and the prime minister were living in open adultery, laborers sold their wives in the market, and fornication was normal. Theaters reveled in producing indecent plays and the literature of the day was steeped in filth, from the gross obscenity of Fielding to the snide nastiness of Sterne. A third characteristic of society was cruelty. There were 253 hanging offenses on the Stature book, and public executions were a major entertainment. Bulls were bedecked with fireworks; these were ignited and the bulls let loose for the amusement of the people. Cockfighting to the death, bearbaiting, and the torture of animals were all popular. On top of all this, it was the great age of the highwaymen. These were criminal gangs, and they engaged in ruthless robbery for the sheer hell of it.

To what extent was the church salt and light in a society as corrupt as this? The answer must be, "Not at all." Rationalism and absenteeism were its main characteristics. The more educated clergy hated "enthusiasm" and believed in God as a disinterested rational being. They paid little attention to Scripture or indeed to Jesus. What's more, they paid little attention to the parishes entrusted to them. Rectors did not usually live in their parishes, and many held multiple benefices that they never visited. They enjoyed their salaries but not their work. Instead, the curates would ride out on a Sunday morning, gabble through the service, and ride on to the next church. Many churches did not even own a Bible or Prayer Book and held but one service a month. Others were in disrepair with shattered windows and broken roof. But nobody cared. The country was coarse, drunken, and lawless while the church was lazy and complacent. The leading theologian of the day, Bishop Joseph Butler, wrote, "It is come . . . to be taken for granted, by many persons, that Christianity is not so much as a subject of inquiry; but that it is, now at length, discovered to be fictitious." Such was England in the early eighteenth century. But the whole situation was utterly transformed within a generation.

The agents of the change were John Wesley and George Whitefield.

CHAPTER 8

The Holy Club

It is fascinating to reflect that if the Rev. Samuel Wesley and his wife, Susanna, had completed their family with fourteen children, the history of the world would have been different. But they had more children, among them John and Charles. Their home was destroyed by a fire, and this made an indelible impression on the eight-year-old John, who later loved to refer to himself as a "brand plucked from the burning" (Zechariah 3:2). He was very religious and when studying at Oxford he, Charles, and some friends started what their mockers called the Holy Club, where they met regularly to read the Greek New Testament. They were exceedingly disciplined, reviewed their lives daily, visited in the prison, and sought to stack up merit with God. Their latest recruit was George Whitefield, the son of a Gloucester innkeeper. He was even more excessive than they in his fasts and acts of self-denial, at times kneeling all night praying in the rain. He stumbled across the idea of "new birth" in a book and knew he needed it. Then, reading another devotional book in his room and reflecting on the crucifixion, he cried out, as Jesus had done, "I thirst." It was a cry of utter helplessness. He realized that he could never work his way to God but that Christ had done all that was necessary for his acceptance. He experienced the new birth for which he longed, and he exclaimed, "Joy unspeakable." The story goes that he ran downstairs and embraced the college porter in his joy!

Failure and New Life

Soon the Holy Club members graduated and left Oxford. The Wesleys went as missionaries to Georgia, and George to a curacy before following them to America. John Wesley's missionary work in America was a disaster. He returned to England deeply depressed, and he was struck by the deep peace Moravian passengers in the boat demonstrated when a fierce storm struck, peace of which he knew nothing. "I came here to convert the Indians," he wrote in his journal, "but O God, who shall convert me?" Not long afterwards he reluctantly accepted an invitation to a Moravian religious meeting in London's Aldersgate Street. Someone was reading from Luther's *Preface to the Epistle to the Romans*. As he listened, Wesley grasped the central truth of the gospel for himself. "I felt my heart strangely warmed," he wrote. "I felt I did trust Christ alone for salvation, and an assurance was given me that he had taken away my sins, even mine." And on that day, May 24, 1738, this dedicated, intellectual, but spiritually blind cleric discovered for himself that new birth which his brother Charles and George Whitefield had experienced a little earlier.

Agents of Revival

Perhaps January 1739 marked the start of the amazing revival that soon swept the country. Whitefield, back from America in order to raise funds for his orphanage in Georgia, was ordained priest in that month, and he and the Wesleys went to a prayer meeting in Fetter Lane. John Wesley described it like this: "About three in the morning as we were continuing instant in prayer, the power of God came mightily upon us, insomuch that many cried out for exceeding joy, and many fell to the ground. As soon as we were recovered a little from that awe and amazement at the presence of his majesty, we broke out with one voice, 'We praise thee, O God; we acknowledge thee to be the Lord.'" That extraordinary prayer meeting was the start of the revival.

There had been partial precedents. The Puritans had emphasized the need for personal repentance and holy living, and some of their works, particularly John Bunyan's *Pilgrim's Progress*, were widely read. The Moravians, with their strong emphasis on personal conversion, though they mainly worked on the continent, had a lively mission in England, and they strongly influenced John Wesley. But most of all, the Great Awakening in America under Jonathan Edwards had begun about ten years earlier. News spread rapidly and led to renewed confidence that God was at work in a fresh way.

Wesley and Whitefield

At all events, Whitefield was a man set free. No longer did he preach grace and works as the ground of salvation, but grace alone. No longer did he read his sermon from a prepared manuscript. He began to preach extempore. No longer did he confine himself to preaching in church. He took to the open air. Barely a month after his profound experience of being filled with the Spirit in Fetter Lane, he saw enormous response to his preaching among the coal miners of Kingswood, Bristol. Soon he was preaching to as many as twenty thousand, and many men were coming to repentance and faith with tears making channels down the grime on their faces. Although most churches were denied them, Whitefield was invited to other cities, including Gloucester and the public parks in London, where at times he spoke to around forty thousand. This is astonishing in a day where there was no public address system. But he wanted to return to the Bristol area, and he asked John Wesley to join him. Before long he had gotten together the necessary funds for his orphanage and returned to America, while entrusting the mission in England to Wesley. John Wesley was at first reluctant to preach in the open air and in someone else's parish, but soon he overcame his scruples, proclaimed that the world was his parish, and continued the work Whitefield had initiated.

Their styles were very different. Whitefield had a magnificent, strong voice and was a natural orator. He appealed to educated circles in the salon of the countess of Huntingdon just as much as he did to the miners, drovers, and fishmongers who never went to church but thronged to hear him in the open air. He spoke directly to the hearts of his hearers and was always talking about the new birth that had transformed his life. Baptism, moral improvement, churchgoing, and religious observance would not get you into the kingdom of God. Only the new birth would suffice, and that is God's sovereign work, but the human conditions are repentance and trust in the finished work of Christ on the cross. A distinguished lady came to hear him preach one morning and he spoke on the text "You must be born again." Fascinated, she returned in the evening and he preached on the same topic. She caught up with him afterwards and asked him why he repeated the same message. His reply reveals his passion and his singlemindedness: "Because, madam, you *must* be born again."

Wesley's preaching was very different. He was an academic, much less demonstrative than Whitefield. He was more precise, preached shorter sermons, and made no pretensions to oratory. He even read his sermons to begin with. But he, too, became fluent in extempore preaching. There was a broad pattern in his evangelistic preaching. To the careless he spoke of death and hell. To those awakened but not yet converted he spoke of repentance and faith. To believers he spoke of the need to press on to "perfection," a developing maturity. Time and again in his journal we read, "I offered them Christ," or "I proclaimed the grace of our Lord Jesus Christ," or "I declared the free grace of God," or "invited all guilty, helpless sinners." Although Whitefield concentrated more on the divine initiative and Wesley more on the need for human response, both preachers were determined not just to impart information like most eighteenth-century preachers but to preach for decision, so that the hearers did not only hear the word of God but felt it and responded to it.

The Message and the Response

For three years they confined themselves to London and the West. Then, with Whitefield in America, Wesley began to ride backward and forward through the whole of England from London to Newcastle, addressing the crowds wherever he could gather them. Wesley tended to ride about forty miles a day and preach in every village through which he passed. This was immensely demanding. One October day in 1739, for instance, he preached at five a.m. to more than two thousand people in Gloucester, at eleven a.m. to a thousand or so in Runwick, and then again in the afternoon. He then rode to Stanley where he preached to about three thousand and then finished the day with another sermon at Ebly. He kept this up for fifty-one years!

The response was mixed. Often the evangelists were mobbed, pelted with refuse, hit with stones or cudgels, and frequently covered in blood. But in spite of this, their success was startling. Wherever Whitefield and the Wesleys went, crowds gathered. The news that God loved them despite what they were like, the fact that Christ had died for each of them personally, and the wonder of free access to this generous God had an immediate and profound effect on the country. The word spread like wildfire. Often people fell to the ground under conviction of sin, contorted with anguish, before they came into the assurance of the new life offered them in Christ. The aim of these evangelists was as simple as it was revolutionary—to save souls and transform lives.

Developments and the Class Meeting

An important feature developed in some of Wesley's urban evangelism. He would travel with a group of about thirty colleagues. Hymns written by Charles would be sung. And after the address the team would move to and fro in the crowd, challenging individuals to respond and inviting them to the class meeting.

The class meeting was the most important way in which Wesley's work proved more permanent than that of Whitefield. New believers were flooding in, and they needed to be looked after. There was the daily five a.m. prayer meeting that played its part, but something more personal and intentional was needed. They were certainly unlikely to get this from their parish churches, although Wesley urged them to worship there as a priority. So something had to be done. Wesley himself wrote, "In a few months, the far greater part of those who had begun to 'fear God and work righteousness,' but were not united together, grew faint in their minds, and fell back into what they were before. Meanwhile the far greater part of those who were thus united together continued 'striving to enter in at the strait gate,' and to 'lay hold on eternal life.'" That was the origin of the class meeting.

Now every Methodist was required not only to attend the parish church but also to meet in class at least once a week. These classes were run by lay people and served a double purpose. On the one hand, they provided nurture and accountability for the new believers; on the other, they were invaluable training grounds for those entrusted with the leadership. These became organized into class leaders, assistants, sick visitors, and stewards. So, by this one move, Wesley went a long way toward solving two of the biggest problems evangelists since him have encountered: the training of assistant leaders and the nurture of new Christians. Soon these houses became too small for the large numbers that came to them, and Wesley was driven to building chapels.

As evidence that Wesley was seeking to remain an Anglican despite most churches rejecting his work, it is worth noting that neither chapels nor informal religious meetings were illegal. It was, of course, at one of the latter that Wesley himself was converted. These class meetings were the brilliant seeds from which the Methodist Church developed, although Wesley remained an Anglican until his death. Most of his converts, however, found the class meetings so helpful and the church services so dreary that a split became inevitable. The converts who stayed within the Church of England became known as Evangelicals, while those who left retained the name of Methodists. At all events, these regular home meetings were invaluable for encouragement, training, and accountability toward attaining the holy life that was one of the main emphases of the movement. It is a great tribute to Wesley's organizational gifts, and the speed with which the revival took hold, that he wrote the conditions for membership of these class meetings on Christmas Day, 1738, less than a year after he himself had discovered a living faith!

It is not surprising that with his emphasis on lay leadership, some laymen began to preach publicly. At first Wesley asked them to stop. But his mother suggested that in so doing he might be resisting the Holy Spirit. Wisely, Wesley listened to his mother, and lay preachers became a regular feature in Methodism, and in due course were gathered into conferences that met annually.

Charles Wesley's Hymns

Open-air preaching and gathering converts into little societies led by laymen were two features of the revival in which Wesley and friends found themselves. But something was missing. You can gather and drill an army, but it needs the inspiration of music before it can march to victory. This was largely provided by Charles Wesley, who produced some of the best hymns in the English language, such as "Jesu, Lover of My Soul," "Oh for a Heart to Praise My God," "Christ the Lord Is Risen Today," "Love Divine, All Loves Excelling," and many more. These were gathered into a hymn book and became not only the musical inspiration but the doctrinal standard of Methodism, which would instill gospel truth and passion into the most uneducated believer.

Holy Living

This chapter has perforce only been a cursory glance at the Evangelical Revival. We have not followed Whitefield to America where his most outstanding impact was made during the Great Awakening. We have not looked at other great leaders, such as William Romaine, Henry Venn, William Grimshaw, and many others who worked alongside Wesley or were inspired by him. We have not looked at the doctrinal differences that divided Wesley from Whitefield, or examined his doctrine of perfection. But there is one area that must be mentioned, as it remains so important for the credibility of any evangelist. It was their lifestyle. Both Wesley and Whitefield were outstanding in their search for a holy life. No scandal ever stuck to either of them. Wesley gave away most of his income to the poor, and Whitefield invested his in the orphanage. They preached holiness of life and they embodied it.* Moreover, what they taught and embodied was characteristic

*Publisher's note: Recent scholarship that the author was unable to take into account has drawn attention to ways in which Whitefield's godliness coexisted with an unwitting entanglement in unholy elements of the imperial regime under which he lived. For example, the orphanage that he sponsored used the labor of enslaved people. See Peter Choi, *George Whitefield: Evangelist for God and Empire* (Grand Rapids: Eerdmans, 2018).

of Methodists up and down the country. In the secular writer W. E. H. Lecky's *History of England in the Eighteenth Century*, we read this: "The doctrines [the Methodist teacher] taught, the theory of life he enforced, proved themselves capable of arousing in great masses of men an enthusiasm of piety which was hardly surpassed in the first days of Christianity, of eradicating inveterate vice, of fixing and directing impulsive and tempestuous natures that were rapidly hastening towards the abyss. . . . [Methodism] placed a fervid and enduring religious sentiment in the minds of the most brutal and most neglected portions of the population." It might be added that Methodism declined when it lost this passion for reaching the poor, and when it abandoned its class meetings.

What are the elements that stand out in this mighty revival, the greatest England has ever known?

1. The discovery that being religious and self-disciplined is not the same as being a Christian. The new birth is essential. A church will achieve nothing without born-again ministers.
2. The emphasis on the work and power of the Holy Spirit. This revival in England was matched by one in America, and spiritual gifts that had long lain dormant reasserted themselves. Wesley was strong on the prevenient work of the Spirit before anyone could come to repentance, and on the fruit of the Spirit in changed lives that followed conversion.
3. The wonderful truth of the free grace of God to sinners who repent and believe was unearthed afresh from the debris of a church lost in formalism and apathy.
4. The willingness to do something new, such as open-air preaching, class meetings, and lay leadership.
5. The willingness to be exhausted in the cause of the gospel and to suffer humiliation, persecution, and physical harm.
6. The importance of partnership, lay involvement, and music in effective evangelism.

7. The disciplined follow-up, nurture, and training of new believers.
8. The godly lifestyle of the leaders that commended their message.
9. The importance of good organization.

For Reflection

1. Am I happy to work in evangelism alongside or under other evangelists?
2. Do I prefer to operate solo or with a team? Why?
3. How far do I understand and adapt the power of contemporary secular music?
4. How far would my lifestyle escape censure by a dispassionate observer?
5. As an evangelist, am I content to count professions of faith, or do I organize new believers into a nurture group?
6. How seriously do I take the need for the Holy Spirit's work in people coming to faith, and his gifts as well as his graces of character?
7. Am I prepared to innovate and have my innovations checked?
8. When did I last engage in open-air preaching?
9. Am I content if people come to church, or do I preach the need for new birth?

9

Eighteenth- and Nineteenth-Century Initiatives

The fruits of the Evangelical Revival affected the whole country, and the later part of the eighteenth and the early nineteenth centuries make that very plain. Out of this wealth of material I propose to look at just four initiatives, very significant in themselves, and all relevant as we consider evangelism in our own day.

Imaginative Evangelistic Clergy

As we have seen, after the death of John Wesley, Methodism separated from the Church of England, and those "enthusiasts" who remained in the Church took the name of Evangelicals. That was an appropriate name since the passion of their lives was the evangel (good news or gospel). They had no new or distinctive doctrines. They simply sought to be faithful to the teaching of the Bible. But it was hard going. Whereas the Methodists were by now well provided with buildings in London, for a long time the only one within the Established Church was St. Dunstan's. Here William Romaine, who was merely the "lecturer," had to contend with clever and sustained opposition for many years before he became known as the most celebrated preacher and evangelist in the city. The Church of England on the whole was hostile to these enthusiasts who preached the grace of God, the atoning cross of Christ, and the importance of faith issuing in a transformed life. Bishops and clergy preferred formal services (conducted no more often than strictly necessary) and a dull and conventional morality. But there was someone they could neither ignore nor silence. Lady Huntingdon, the daughter of one earl and wife of another, could appoint her own chaplains and use her various homes in London and elsewhere for spiritual meetings. She was a great supporter of Whitefield himself, and he would often address a scintillating array of nobility and even royalty in her London mansion. She sold her jewels to finance chaplains to preach the gospel, particularly to her own class in society, which sorely needed it. In the end, constant opposition led her to abandon the Church of England and to found her independent Countess of Huntingdon's Connexion, which still exists in a small way today.

In other parts of the country, clergy who were gripped by the awakening toiled away at spreading the faith. Up in Yorkshire, William Grimshaw was a colorful evangelist. He was vicar of Haworth, a village that seemed to have lapsed into open paganism. But Grimshaw was as tough, fearless, and strong-willed as the best of them. He managed to stop Sunday football and get most of the village into church, where his prayers were memorable. As Erasmus Middleton put it, "He was like a man with his feet on earth and his soul in heaven." He would intersperse his own comments into the reading of Scripture, all delivered in broad Yorkshire, and while the psalm before the sermon was being sung, he took a whip into the streets and drove any idlers he found into church! He was a powerful preacher, strong on the cross of Christ, yet full of racy humor, which his audience appreciated. He used to boast that he always preached "in market language," something unusual among the clergy of his day.

Another great northern evangelist was Henry Venn of Huddersfield. Like Grimshaw, he spent much of his time on horseback, reaching out to obscure parishioners in lonely farms and cottages. He drew enormous congregations that often overflowed the capacity of the church. And then he took to preaching in the open air. He had the gift of moving thousands to repentance and tears. Charles Simeon, to whom we shall turn below, wrote of him, "The only end for which he lived was to make all men see the glory of God in the face of Jesus Christ." He was blessed with great common sense, and people often sought his advice: but behind it all he was seeking to lead them to Christ. He wrote a significant book, *Complete Duty of Man*, which dealt with the common difficulties people experience, and he handled them in a way that constantly pointed to Christ. This book was timely and percolated into many parts of the country.

Fletcher of Madeley in the Severn valley provides another example of the best sort of eighteenth-century evangelist. He was known for his saintly character, and although the large village of Madeley was every bit as dissolute and heathen as Grimshaw's, Fletcher loved the people and stayed there for twenty-five years, resisting not only all offers of preferment but also Wesley's suggestion that he should become an itinerant evangelist. The tiny congregation he found soon grew and overflowed the church: indeed, a windowpane was removed near the pulpit so that people could stand in the churchyard and hear the sermon! But a crowded church was not enough for Fletcher. He started Sunday schools for the children and in the summer held services in the woods. Every weekday a service was held in some part of the parish, and he gathered those who responded into home groups where he gave careful instruction. But his greatest gift seems to have been in personal evangelism. He was very skilled at drawing lessons from everyday life. To the woman whose market basket he was carrying he spoke of one who died to bear a heavier burden for her. To the farmer with his gun he spoke of sin as missing the mark. When chatting with a woman who was sweeping the floor, he asked if she took as great care in cleaning up the mess in her life. This gift of natural, one-to-one evangelism is one that can be learned, if we take the trouble.

Then there was John Newton, the converted slave trader who in due course was ordained. He worked in Olney, a large Buckinghamshire village, inhabited, as he wrote, "by the half-starved and ragged of the earth." Not only did he cooperate closely with William Wilberforce on the slavery issue, but he was a gifted evangelist and an outstanding hymn writer. He composed many hymns for his midweek prayer meeting, some of which, like "Amazing Grace," we sing today.

But these men, and there was a fair sprinkling of them, were exceptions, and on the whole the country was spiritually dark in the decades that followed Wesley and Whitefield. The king, George III, was insane. America had recently rebelled against British rule. The French Revolution sent terror into English hearts—they knew that the same could happen here. Unitarianism, belief in God but not in the distinctive truths of Christianity, was the prevailing creed among many educated people, and the masses were sunk in ignorance and dissolute habits. These were dark days. Nevertheless, these heroic, evangelistic clergy showed that the gospel had its ancient power and could still transform individuals and society.

The Clapham Sect, Wilberforce, and the Slave Trade

The gospel preached by Wesley and Whitefield would have been a poor thing had it not changed social attitudes in eighteenth- and early-nineteenth-century England. Would the movement fade away into pietism or become a strong and enduring feature in society? The answer lay in a remarkable group of gifted laymen, known as the Clapham Sect since they lived in what was then the small village of Clapham adjoining London. They included Henry Thornton the banker; Charles

Grant, chairman of the East India Company; Zachary Macau-
lay, governor of Sierra Leone; Lord Teignmouth, who had
been governor-general of India; and William Wilberforce.
They were a power in the land.

Perhaps the most significant of them all was Wilberforce.
Born in 1759, he was small and sickly and had shown little sign
of spiritual interest until his conversion while on a tour of Europe at the age of twenty-one. By then he had gained a seat in
parliament while still an undergraduate. His conversion transformed his life and attitudes. He would spend three hours
in prayer and Bible study each day. He was immensely self-
disciplined and generous with his money, and he brought his
Christianity into his politics, where he gained the reputation
of being the greatest orator in the House. When he discovered the terrible conditions in which slaves were transported
from Africa to America and the ghastly cruelties inflicted on
them in the plantations, he was deeply concerned. This was
a massive and profitable trade, very popular among the rich
merchants of England and America. It would be immensely
difficult to stop. He was slow to take up the cudgels on their
behalf, waiting modestly for someone more distinguished to
do so, but in 1787 at the instigation of his friend William Pitt,
the prime minister, he started a sustained antislavery campaign that lasted until his death. The opposition was bound to
be enormous because so many people invested very profitably
in the trade. More than two hundred English ships sailed from
Bristol to carry on the trade. They raided African villages and
transported men, women, and children to America to work in
the plantations. The conditions on the long voyage were horrendous. Apparently one and a half million, of the total eleven
million transported to America, died during the voyage. This
had been going on for years and even good, sensitive men like
Whitefield saw nothing wrong with it. But Wilberforce and
his friends in the Clapham Sect set themselves to wipe out this
inhuman trade. The ship owners, the merchants, the finan-

ciers, and the plantation owners were all up in arms. The king was firmly against the Clapham group, seeing them as revolutionaries planning a reign of terror. Lord Nelson inveighed passionately against "the damnable doctrine of Wilberforce and his hypocritical allies."

Throughout all this opposition, Wilberforce strove valiantly in parliament. Eleven times an antislavery bill was introduced into parliament, and eleven times it was debated and defeated. The struggle lasted twenty years. The public had to be educated, witnesses had to be gathered, petitions organized, committees attended, debates won. His friends in the Clapham Sect agreed each to give up a night's sleep once a week in order to sift all the evidence that was pouring in. Outside parliament, Wilberforce had a doughty supporter in John Newton who had himself been captain of a slave ship for some years even after his conversion. Once he was convinced it was wrong, he became a great support to Wilberforce. The slave trade was made illegal in Britain in 1807. But the struggle had broken Wilberforce's health. Nevertheless, he lived to see the day, just before his death, when all slaves were set free and slavery was banished in the entire British empire.

Nobody could deny that the chief agent in this remarkable achievement was Wilberforce, and nobody could deny that it was his evangelical Christian faith which drove him to such sustained labor. The faith that had led the slave owner Philemon to welcome back his runaway slave Onesimus, no longer as a slave but as a brother (Philemon 16), drove Wilberforce to see all these slaves as his brothers, deserving the respect due to every human being. And by this action he inaugurated a great step forward in evangelism. It demonstrated the essential link between proclamation and social concern. Freeing the slaves led to the conversion of a great many of them, and also of many in England whose consciences had hitherto been blighted by tolerating such a foul trade. The apostle Paul had insisted that faith must show itself in works, and it certainly did through this outstanding work of Wilberforce and his friends.

Wilberforce has rightly been acclaimed as one of the greatest humanitarian heroes Britain has ever produced. But he did not do it on his own. His endurance and single-mindedness were nourished by his daily devotional time with God and by the support and encouragement of his friends in the Clapham Sect. These were, as we have seen, wealthy, influential men who were as effective in reaching the upper classes in society as the Methodists were among the poor. People scornfully mocked them as the "saints" but were unaware of the very self-disciplined lives they led and the fact that they gave away far more of their income than they retained for themselves. The sheer companionship and mutual affection of this group led to far more than any one of them, Wilberforce included, could have achieved on their own. They established and financed hospitals, began schools for the poor, the blind, and the deaf, paid for the release of imprisoned debtors, set up lending libraries, and started a society for preventing cruelty to animals. They spread their convictions in a new journal, *The Christian Observer*, which was much cheaper than any other on the market and soon gained a large circulation. The contributors were mainly Clapham men, and because of their intimate business knowledge of many parts of the world, their material was always accurate and enlightening. Overseas they played a major part in the founding of Freetown in Sierra Leone. It was the first British colony in Africa, and it was established with three aims—the abolition of the slave trade, the civilization of Africa, and the introduction of the gospel. They were also influential in the founding of the Church Missionary Society for ministry abroad and prepared the way for the Church Pastoral Aid Society to serve the urban needs thrown up by the industrial revolution in England. Both are still very effective today.

It would be no exaggeration to say that the Clapham Sect changed the face of England in their day. They provide an

outstanding example of what can be achieved in the further-
ance of the gospel both in word and deed when a group of
dedicated and gifted Christian friends commit themselves
single-mindedly to the cause.

Charles Simeon and Church Leadership

A remarkable man was born in Reading in 1759: Charles Simeon, who in the course of his life achieved an influence unri-
valed by any archbishop. He went up to King's College, Cambridge, as a wild tearaway, known for his love of extravagant
dress and horses. But shortly after his arrival, he was informed
by the Provost that, because of some ancient rule, he must attend Holy Communion in chapel three weeks later. Reflecting
that the devil was as fit for Communion as he, he acquired a
book about it that led to his conversion. He entrusted his life
to Christ and at once the effects began to be seen. He started
to study the Scriptures and apply them to his way of life. At
the early age of twenty-three, he was ordained and became
a Fellow of Kings, and the next year he also became vicar of
Holy Trinity, a church in the city center, where he stayed for
the rest of his life. The congregation, who wanted someone
else, made his life a misery and for years locked the box pews
in the main part of the church against him. He had to preach
to the side aisles, which soon became very full. Accordingly,
for more than ten years most of his congregation had to stand.
He also sustained a lot of opposition and abuse from rowdy
students. But politely and persistently he carried out his work
and in due course became recognized as the best preacher in
Cambridge. He was very earnest. There was no embellish-
ment, no ostentation, but clear, attractive presentation of
the great truths of the gospel, accompanied by powerful and
appropriate gestures. He had a distinguished career at King's,
holding the offices of dean, bursar, and vice-provost, but he

was appreciated as much by the poor and unlettered as he was by the intelligent. The story is told by H. C. G. Moule, in his book *Charles Simeon*, of an old man, John Munn, who had once heard Simeon when he went preaching in the "'Fen-country,' and often afterwards he craved to hear him again. Every now and then he would say, . . . 'That's the man as touches my heart! Can't he just preach! . . .' And off he would go, tramping the fifty miles to Cambridge" from Northampton where he lived.

Simeon loved to expound Scripture and his approach to it was both reverent and scrupulously honest. "My endeavour," he said, "is to bring out of Scripture what is there, and not to thrust in what I think might be there. I have a great jealousy on this head; never to speak more or less than I believe to be the mind of the Spirit in the passage I am expounding." He avoided emotionalism like the plague, and yet his preaching often deeply stirred the emotions. Living as he did in the midst of great controversy about divine election and human free will, topics that had divided Whitefield and Wesley, he preserved a superb balance. He showed that both are taught, and he maintained that the truth lies neither in one extreme nor in the other, nor yet in a mean between the two, but by holding firmly to both at the same time. God's election is real. But so is human response to his gracious initiative. This balance, this passion, this clarity was rare in Cambridge in Simeon's day and still is. Unsurprisingly, he packed not only his own church but the nearby Great St. Mary's, where he was often invited as the years went on. A friend wrote, "The sight of the overflowing church was almost electric," and on another occasion, "There was scarcely room to move."

But preaching was not the only way Simeon set about evangelism. He ran weekly Friday tea parties in his rooms in Kings and people could come and ask him anything they liked. He took great trouble to help ordinands to grasp the great truths of the faith and learn how to proclaim them effectively. His celebrated sermon class trained most of the best preachers of the next generation. All this continued for some fifty years! It would be hard to exaggerate his influence on English society.

He had a great passion for spreading the gospel to the heathen. His concern for bringing the gospel to India can be traced back to within four years of his appointment at Holy Trinity. For some years the Eclectic Society, composed of young evangelical clergy whom he gathered together, had been wondering how to bring the gospel to Africa and the East Indies. Then early in 1799, while the French Revolution was raging, Simeon posed three significant questions to the Eclectics. They were, "What can we do? When shall we do it? How shall we do it?" They determined to found a society immediately for "missions to Africa and the East" and the Church Missionary Society was formed immediately by a mere twenty-five people, with John Venn as chairman and Henry Thornton as treasurer. Young evangelical chaplains were appointed to the East India Company and sought to minister both to its employees and to the native population. One of these chaplains, who had been deeply stirred by a sermon of Simeon's, was Henry Martyn, a brilliant mathematician and fellow of his Cambridge college. He was a gifted linguist and soon became skilled in Sanskrit, Persian, and Arabic. He translated the New Testament into Urdu, Persian, and Hindustani, but he died of fever in 1812 at the age of thirty-one. His motto was "Let me burn out for God." Burn out he did.

Simeon and his friends in the Clapham Sect had a worldwide concern, and under their aegis missionaries also went to Canada, the Cape, Botany Bay in Australia, and Sierra Leone. It is no exaggeration to say that the Anglican Communion, that is to say, the network of churches around the world that are allied to the Church of England, owes its origin to the Church Missionary Society, and to the man whose pregnant questions to the Eclectics in 1799 led to its inauguration.

One other aspect of Simeon's ministry must be mentioned. He was much troubled that good men like William Romaine and John Newton remained unbeneficed almost to the end of their lives, while so many lazy and ineffective clergy enjoyed rich livings. He determined to do something about it. So, using some money left him by his brother's death, he bought up the right to appoint a clergyman as rector of a parish. "Others . . . purchase income," he said, "but I purchase spheres [of influence]." Friends and supporters produced further funds, and the Simeon Trustees, two hundred years later, now look after and control the appointment of more than a hundred parishes, many of them in very significant places. I had the privilege of working in one of them, St. Aldate's in the heart of Oxford. This was a brilliant move of Simeon's, as it ensured the continuance of evangelical ministry and pastoral care in these parishes.

Shaftesbury the Reformer

The criterion for authentic evangelism is not whether it increases the numbers in church, nor whether it makes a person more moral, but whether it impacts society for good. It is fascinating to trace the way the spiritual renewal in England developed. The first phase of the great Evangelical Revival under Wesley, Whitefield, and their colleagues brought countless people face to face with God. The second phase under the Clapham Sect began to change abuses in society and to pioneer foreign missions. The third phase was led by Shaftesbury, the outstanding reformer of the Victorian age. It has been said that almost all the best Christian philanthropic work in that period can be attributed to this remarkable man who became known as "the poor man's earl." Though he lived somewhat later than the Clapham group (1801–1885), he very much shared their vision, and it is instructive to glance at some of the achievements of his long life if we are to see the genuine outworking of the revival that had begun several decades earlier.

Anthony Ashley Cooper, known as Lord Ashley until 1851 when he succeeded his father and became the seventh Earl of Shaftesbury, had a wealthy but unhappy childhood. His aristocratic parents were aloof and gave him little love. The person who really cared for him in those early years was a wonderful maid, Maria Millis. She had clearly been reached by the awakening and she loved the lad, taught him the stories of the Bible and how to pray, and led his young heart to Christ. He was sent to school at Harrow, and when he was sixteen he was confronted by an incident that changed his life. He was walking down Harrow Hill when he saw four drunken men lurching down the street, carrying the coffin of a dead pauper. They stumbled before reaching the churchyard, dropped the coffin, and let out a stream of oaths. Ashley was sickened by the sight of a fellow human being taken to his grave with nobody to mourn him, and his corpse treated with derision by these drunk men who cared nothing. Looking back on the event, he saw it as the motivation for his public career. "[It] brought powerfully before me the scorn and neglect manifested towards the Poor and helpless. . . . I was convinced that God had called me to devote whatever advantages he might have bestowed upon me, to the cause of the weak, the helpless, both man and beast, and those who had none to help them." This resolve led him into parliament. He did not have an easy ride. His fellow Tories did not share his concerns for the poor, and like Wilberforce before him, he had to fight constant battles as he sought to improve their lot.

First, he turned his attention to those suffering from mental illness. Nobody understood this ailment or attempted to provide medication. Instead, the lunatics were regarded as a public nuisance and treated as criminals. They were kept in institutions, slept on straw, and at weekends were chained to their pallets, where they had to wallow in their own excrement. On Mondays they were put in a big tub of cold water, in all weathers, and mopped down like animals. One towel sufficed for more than a hundred of them. Ashley began regular visits to these asylums to see the conditions for himself. This enabled him to speak powerfully in parliament and bring about reform. He cared deeply for these unfortunates, and he became chair of the Lunacy Commissioners whom parliament appointed, a post he held for fifty-seven years.

He then set about trying to rectify the worst abuses brought about by the industrial revolution. Children as young as five were taken from the London workhouses to work in stifling conditions in the factories for as much as fourteen hours a day. Down the mines it was even worse. Ashley found this intolerable, but the opposition he faced was massive. The mill owners and mine owners had enormous influence in the House and maintained that the wealth of the country would be destroyed if parliament interfered. He brought in bill after bill, but they were voted down until, after seventeen years of unremitting effort, he secured the passing of the Factories Acts, which swept away the worst of these evils.

Throughout his long career he was quick to notice abuses and then to effect improvements. He saw a small boy carrying rods and brushes on his back, ready to climb naked up inside chimneys to clean them. He saw small children being forced to work in the fields. He saw children covered with wet clay being driven toward the kilns in the brickfields. All these situations he was eventually able to change. He loved children and was able to inaugurate "ragged schools" offering free education for the poorest children, which were staffed by volunteers. The list of organizations for the relief of those in need that he founded or presided over is extensive and includes the Royal Society for the Prevention of Cruelty to Animals, North London Homes for the Blind, the National

Anti-vivisection Society, Barnardo's, the Association for the Disabled, the YMCA, the YWCA, the National Society for the Prevention of Cruelty to Children, and many others. All of this was the outworking of his strong evangelical faith. It was his very practical way of spreading the gospel of Jesus and emphasizing his compassion for the poor and needy. He proclaimed himself "an evangelical of the evangelicals" and was unashamed about it. His evangelistic zeal led him to inaugurate the Church's Ministry among the Jews, the London City Mission, the Missions to Seamen, the Dean Close School, and the Church Pastoral Aid Society. This last, founded in 1836, was particularly significant. Every year, according to government statistics, more than one hundred thousand people moved from the countryside to the factory towns. This, of course, put them outside the parish system that had existed in England from time immemorial. Many of them lived in abject misery and had no religious support. He longed for "the Church of England . . . [to] dive into the recesses of human misery and bring out the wretched and ignorant sufferers to bask in the light, and life, and liberty of the gospel." So he and friends set up the Church Pastoral Aid Society to increase the number of working clergy and to appoint godly laymen to work with them. His concern for the spread of the gospel overseas through his beloved Church Missionary Society was thus matched by his determination to reach the needy in this country with the gospel that had changed his own life.

It is not surprising that one of the biggest crowds ever seen in London attended his funeral in Westminster Abbey. His son records, "When I saw the crowd which lined the streets . . . , the halt, the blind, the maimed, the poor and naked standing bare-headed in their rags amidst a pelting rain patiently enduring to show their love and reverence to their departed friend, I thought it the most heart-stirring sight my eyes had ever looked upon."

For Reflection

1. Do I share the courage and directness of these eighteenth-century evangelists?
2. Do I work consistently for a lifetime goal like Wilberforce and Shaftesbury?
3. Do I care for the salvation of those I have never seen, as these men did?
4. Is my evangelism merely verbal, or do I engage in actions that display the good news?
5. Do I partner with others to effect that change in society to which evangelism leads?

10

The Welsh Revival

The Welsh Revival in 1904 and 1905 was the greatest spiritual movement the little principality of Wales has ever experienced. Even now, people in Wales are very aware of it and look back either with fond gratitude or scornful disapproval. There is no doubt that it was highly divisive. No doubt either that it affected vast numbers of people, most of whom had previously had nothing to do with religion. It is well worth studying, for it embodies some unusual factors in evangelism.

The Situation in Wales

Most of the reforms inaugurated by Shaftesbury had passed Wales by. The majority of the population were desperately poor, but Wales had long been a land of song, poetry, rugby football, and short-term religious revivals. But the story started earlier in another land. In 1858 a remarkable outbreak of corporate prayer took place in America. It began when a businessman, Jeremiah Lanphier, sensing the economic depression of the day, distributed leaflets announcing a midday hour of prayer on a Wednesday. On the first occasion he was the only one present for most of the hour, but finally he was joined by five other businessmen. The next week there were twenty, the following week forty. They decided to meet daily instead of weekly, and soon prayer meetings were springing up throughout the city. Before long, some fifty thousand people seem to have been involved.

It was the precursor to the 1859 revival that reached a million people in America and Canada and spread to most of the world, including Wales, where Dafydd Morgan, a Calvinistic Methodist preacher, went to bed "a lamb" and woke up "a lion." For a short time he had a remarkable evangelistic ministry up and down Wales. The country was not unused to such periodic spiritual eruptions. But they tended to die down quickly and none of them remotely matched what happened in 1904. This was extremely well documented because it attracted great attention in the press, and it was remarkable for several reasons. For one thing, it was a spontaneous outburst of the Holy Spirit: there was no organization, no central leadership, no direction. For another, it mainly affected two denominations: the Congregationalists and the Calvinistic Methodists. It began in the mining communities of South Wales, but it soon engulfed the country. The language of the revival was Welsh.

The spiritual position in Wales was dire. Many of the people were entirely untouched by Christianity, and the pastors had become increasingly dismissive of orthodoxy, not least because of the publication of Darwin's *Origin of Species* and William James's *The Varieties of Religious Experience*, which saw conversion as a temporary psychological phenomenon. German higher criticism was at its height, and all this discredited faith in Scripture as divine revelation. Thus, a lack of confidence spread widely among the pastors and even entered the Sunday schools. In a word, the religious climate was cold. Nobody could have anticipated the revival that soon swept the country.

There were, of course, faithful clergy and men and women of prayer. A Welsh offshoot of the Keswick Convention, designed to promote biblical holiness, took place in Llandrindod Wells in Central Wales, and it profoundly affected Joseph Jenkins, a minister in the village of New Quay, and his nephew John Thickens, minister in Aberaeron. They began to experience considerable fruitfulness in their work, particularly among the youth, some of whom went on "missionary journeys" to other churches. Then in September 1904, the Rev. Seth Joshua came to New Quay for a mission, and he was delighted to see signs of God's work there already, which gave him a platform for an unusual and very successful mission. The presence of God's Spirit was palpable, the testimonies powerful, the worship electric. Many came to faith, some of them crying aloud. Joshua sensed that revival was in the air and moved on to another village, Newcastle Emlyn, accompanied by a team of enthusiastic youngsters from New Quay. It was here that Evan Roberts, a young man of twenty-six, first heard Joshua and was deeply impressed. Roberts would soon become central in the revival.

Evan Roberts

Evan Roberts was a serious-minded young Christian who spent three or more hours in Bible study and prayer each day. He was a coal miner, like his father. He had started down the mine at the age of eleven and worked there until he was twenty-three, when he joined his uncle, a blacksmith, for fifteen months before giving in to his longstanding urge to be a preacher of the gospel. Newcastle Emlyn was the place where the Calvinistic Methodists trained their ministers, and he enrolled as a student in 1904. Joshua was critical of the heavy emphasis on academic study at the college, and its weakness in the area of spiritual formation and practical experience. So Roberts, after seeking permission from his tutor, joined him and his team as they went to Blaenannerch, where further meetings had been planned. During one of the prayer meetings, Roberts burst out with a heartfelt prayer, as he reflected on God's great love: he cried out, "Bend me, bend me. Bend us," and fell prostrate on the floor. This caused no small stir, and those words became almost the motto of the revival: "Bend the church and save the world." At all events, Roberts was filled with peace after his outburst and saw it as a turning point in his life: he called it his "baptism in the Holy Spirit." He became convinced that he must preach the gospel throughout Wales. His devotional life was remarkable. He tells how one night in 1904 he woke at one a.m. and had four hours of intense communion with God. This became a regular pattern (until he entered the theological college!), and he was given assurance in a vision that no less than one hundred thousand people would be won for Christ. This in fact happened during the remarkable revival in the autumn of 1904 until the spring of 1905. That great number did come to a dynamic faith, although many of them perished in World War I just ten years later.

Roberts soon began to play a crucial part in the revival, though it had no central organization and broke out spontaneously throughout the land. There was no planning, and no individuals could claim leadership of the movement: it was a sovereign outbreak of the Spirit of God, apparently at random wherever people were praying and longing for a fresh touch of God's power. But Roberts was an important part of it. This is all the more remarkable since he had little formal education, though he loved books, and he had been a coal miner for twelve years. But Evan Roberts was a remarkable man: humble, gracious, warm, intelligent, with a strong personality, something of a mystic, he did not fit into any normal ministerial pattern. He was one of a kind. He had an intense awareness of the Holy Spirit and his guidance, and he was often given remarkable visions that directed his actions. He frequently spoke of them. Once he saw multitudes going down a slope to the bottomless pit. In anguish he cried out to God to close the door to hell for one year, to give them time to respond. On another occasion he saw a hand, which he took to be the hand of God, holding a piece of paper with the number 100,000 on it. His return to Loughor was prompted by a repeated vision of his standing before his mates in the schoolroom and a voice saying to him, "Go and speak to these people." That is why he reluctantly returned to his home village, gathered his schoolfellows, and began to speak. It was hard going. But at length six responded and came out to the front to confess Christ. He agonized for others, and gradually another six took the same step. But none of the others. Before long his family entered this vital awareness of the presence of God, and so did several young people from the neighborhood. Numbers rocketed, and soon drew the attention of the press. A journalist from the *Western Mail*, the main newspaper of Wales, was sent to report on one of these meetings. He was much impressed and wrote as follows:

> The preacher did not remain in his seat. For the most part he walked up and down the aisles, open Bible in hand, exhorting one, encouraging another, and kneeling with a third to implore a blessing from the Throne of Grace. A young woman rose to give out a hymn, which was sung with deep earnestness. While it was being sung, several people dropped down in their seats as if they had been struck, and commenced crying for pardon. Then from another part of the chapel could be heard the voice of a young man reading a portion of scripture. Finally, Mr. Roberts announced the holding of further meetings, and at 4:25 [a.m.] the gathering dispersed.

The Meetings

These meetings, which were meant to end at midnight, often invaded the small hours, and they left Roberts with little rest after his extended nighttime prayer before visiting the miners at five a.m. at the pit-head and inviting them to the evening service. This was followed by the first of his three daily services. How he managed to preach when exhausted by this demanding schedule beggars belief. It is often said that his preaching was not particularly remarkable, but his words penetrated to the heart of even the toughest miners in the Rhondda. He spoke in a quiet, intense voice very different from the emotionalism of many revivalists. But on the whole, the preaching did not play a dominant part in the revival. Roberts left each meeting entirely in the hands of the Holy Spirit: he constantly sought to follow the Spirit's guidance. Song, testimonies, verses of Scripture came from all parts of the packed chapels, accompanied by cries for mercy as people fell to the ground, and shouts of joy as they received assurance of God's pardon. Often the meetings began with the five "singing sisters" who had followed him from New Quay—he rarely journeyed without them, and their contribution was significant. Roberts would walk around, trying to discern whom God was particularly touching, and urging them to repent. It was all wonderfully chaotic. An aged Welshman I once knew, who had crept into one of these meetings as a small boy, determined to see what was going on, remarked, "Mad, quite mad." So it would have seemed to many. But to the vast majority of those who attended, it was the greatest experience of God they had ever known. Each day's meetings were recorded not only in the *Western Mail* but in English dailies, and people came from various parts of the world to observe this remarkable phenomenon for themselves.

The Message

Was there anything peculiar about Roberts's message? In one sense, no. He was deeply versed in the Scripture and wholeheartedly believed its doctrine. But in another sense, yes, because he stressed the need for baptism in the Holy Spirit, something that heavily influenced the emerging Pentecostals. He saw this as a vital second stage in the spiritual life after conversion, and there were four essential steps that led to it. The first was confession of all known sin to God and restitution to others. Second was the insistence that any doubtful practice, even if not specifically sinful, must be put away. Third, there must be a prompt and wholehearted obedience to the Holy Spirit. And fourth, there must be fearless public confession of Christ as Savior and Lord. This was the message that he and his colleagues in the revival insisted on time and again. They saw it as the gateway to baptism in the Holy Spirit. It was, they claimed, no innovation but a return to the Pentecost sermon at the very start of Christianity.

A notable feature of the Welsh Revival was that Evan Roberts refused to be treated as a celebrity, declined invitations overseas, and insisted that it was not his revival in any sense but the sovereign work of the Holy Spirit of God. This was borne out by the fact that the revival broke out in various parts of Wales where he was not present. But his humility was unusual. It is all too easy for a leader to claim credit in the midst of a notable work of God. He refused to do so. Moreover, whereas many evangelists make a good deal of money, Evan Roberts gave most of his away. Yet for a few months from November 1904 until the spring of 1905, he was one of the most celebrated people in the world.

Opposition—and Withdrawal

Needless to say, there was opposition. In January 1905 the Rev. Peter Price, a Congregational minister, launched a broadside against Roberts, very publicly in the *Western Mail*. Price claimed that the fruitfulness of his own church was the real revival, whereas what Evan Roberts was involved in was a blasphemous travesty. Price was a Cambridge graduate, with far greater academic firepower than Roberts, and his attack aroused widespread and quite prolonged controversy. He took particular exception to Roberts's claim to operate continually under the direct inspiration and guidance of the Holy Spirit, and he decried the disorder, noise, emotionalism, and physical manifestations in the revival meetings. This opposition, to which Roberts did not reply, hurt him deeply. But his claims to direct obedience to the Holy Spirit intensified. So much so that on one occasion he cried out that a damned soul was present in the meeting: it was no good praying for him, for he was finally damned. This incident made it clear to many that Roberts was becoming deranged. Indeed, by February 1905 he was a nervous wreck. The intense pressure under which he had been working was more than any man could long sustain, and the bitter attack was the last straw. He had a complete mental and physical collapse. He never engaged in any public ministry after 1905, though he lived until 1951, but after many months of recovery in the home of Jessie Penn-Lewis, a colleague in the revival, he left Wales for England and gave himself entirely to prayer for world revival, sometimes for as much as eighteen hours a day. He was convinced that he could do far more by prayer than anything else. But without him the Welsh Revival soon came to an end. It had lasted less than a year but had rocked the nation.

Failings and Strengths of the Revival

How shall we assess this remarkable movement? There were great weaknesses. One was Roberts's increasing obsession with demons. He admitted they were active in his meetings—an admission he later retracted. He and Jessie Penn-Lewis, with whom he stayed for some time after 1905, wrote the book *War on the Saints*, which asserted unprecedented demonic activity during the revival. Was that the case? Or was this obsession the result of his mental and physical exhaustion? His increasingly erratic behavior made that hard to believe. Then there was the emotionalism and disorder in his meetings, accompanied by several doctrinal weaknesses. How biblical was his insistence on the necessity of a second and powerful post-conversion experience of the Holy Spirit? How biblical was his view that the ensuing new dimension of spiritual life led to "entire sanctification"? How biblical was his claim to be constantly acting under the influence of the Holy Spirit? Such a claim can make a person impervious to the advice of others and obstinate in a course of action. These were undeniable failings.

On the other hand, the strengths of the revival were enormous. It was not only the greatest spiritual awakening Wales has ever had, but it triggered other contemporary revivals abroad, including France, Norway, Sweden, Australia, and Patagonia. In 1905 the Welsh missionaries in India witnessed a similar visitation by God among the unemotional Tamils. It is well recorded by the missionary author Amy Carmichael. It would scarcely be an exaggeration to say that the church worldwide was affected by the Welsh Revival during the following decade, as churches and individuals experienced a greater unity, joy, and desire to spread the gospel. The Welsh Revival also had a particularly strong impact on young people and led to an explosion of lay leadership. With fire in their bellies, men prayed together down the mines and on the trains, and they were knit together in a close fellowship that helped to bring about the socialism that has ever since characterized Welsh politics. Moreover, the moral impact of the revival is hard to exaggerate. Wherever the revival broke out crime decreased to such an extent that magistrates sometimes had no cases to try. The pubs were largely forsaken for the prayer meetings, where erstwhile drunks and prize fighters gave their testimony to the power of the Spirit. Drunkenness almost disappeared, and thousands became teetotal. Both hotels and pubs registered a big loss of trade. People took their faith seriously. There was a new integrity in the workplace: employers noted the fresh willingness of their staff to work hard. Character, too, was transformed and old habits broken. One of the amusing tales about the revival is that the pit donkeys no longer understood their masters: instead of thrashing and cursing them, the men were kind and spoke gently. Debts were paid, feuds were healed, and family life was enhanced. The social impact of the revival was enormous for a decade, but by the end of the First World War it had largely disappeared, and today there is no sign of it.

Lessons for Modern Evangelists

What is a modern evangelist to make of this astonishing movement? Perhaps the most important thing is to be open to God working in a way in which the evangelist is not central. Famous preachers such as F. B. Meyer, William Booth, and Campbell Morgan came to observe the revival, and were invited to preach, but all three of them had the wisdom to decline. They were not going to interfere in what was so manifestly a work of God. Roberts himself felt the same, which is why he made no effort to control or steer the meetings. "This movement is not of me, it is of God," he claimed, time and again: "I would not dare to try to direct it." A tendency toward control tends to grow in the successful evangelist. He needs to learn to stand aside when God is at work without him.

Another important lesson for evangelists is that the sermon is not necessarily the most important part of the service. Often Roberts would say almost nothing in these meetings, except perhaps for a few enigmatic sentences, but would go looking for signs of God at work on individuals and seek to help. The singing, the testimonies, the prayers (often several people at once), and the sense of awe in God's presence had a greater effect than his preaching. Indeed, what shocks most evangelists is that he did not prepare his addresses at all. He spoke what he believed God was giving him, and had no idea afterward what he had said. There was prophetic preaching like that in the second century with Melito, bishop of Sardis, but it is rare and cannot be conjured up.

A third great lesson for any would-be evangelist is that academic theological training cannot by itself equip a preacher to reach the souls of men and women. Roberts had no such education, but his passion, his deep study of Scripture, and his walk with God gave him this astonishing impact.

A fourth thing stares us in the face. This man gave himself to extended times of prayer, not primarily for the success of his own ministry but for God to work without hindrance in his beloved Wales. There will be no effective evangelism, let alone another revival, without serious prayer, which is the last thing we want to engage in because it is such hard work.

There is a final point that every evangelist should note. God picked this man up, used him phenomenally for less than a year, and then laid him aside, his work done. Evangelists need to remember they are dispensable, and that is a painful lesson.

For Reflection

1. Would I actually want something as chaotic as a revival, let alone pray for it?
2. If I desire fruit in evangelism, am I willing to give myself to prayer?
3. Am I willing for God either to use me or to lay me aside?

CHAPTER 10

4. Do I believe God can break up really hard, godless soil?

5. Do I see evangelism as primarily a solo affair, or do I make use of a team and a variety of approaches?

6. Am I content for God to do his own work in his own way, not mine?

11

Crusade Evangelism

In February 1837, a baby was born in a humble farmhouse in Northfield, Massachusetts, who was destined to become the greatest evangelist in the nineteenth century. His name was Dwight L. Moody, and it was he who inaugurated what we now know as "crusade evangelism."

Its origins lay in the "revivals" of the American West. In Britain the word "revival" is used of a sovereign break-in by God, such as the Welsh Revival. In America the word is used differently to denote a short, intense evangelistic campaign. As the American frontier moved west after the Revolutionary War, the spiritual needs were met by Methodist circuit riders and Baptist farmer-preachers. But soon "camp meetings" developed. These were open-air gatherings with hymn singing, preaching, and an invitation to come to Christ. Rails were erected near the platform for "seekers," and the meetings (three a day) lasted for three or four days before the revivalist moved on elsewhere. These were not only spiritual but important social gatherings for frontier settlers, many of whom lived in isolated places.

In the East of the United States, these "revivals" tended to be more thoughtful, taking on atheism and deism as well as preaching repentance and faith.

Charles Finney

Undoubtedly the most significant predecessor to Moody was Charles Finney. In 1821 he came to Christ on his own after a day meditating in the forest where he had had a powerful experience of the Holy Spirit. He became a preacher, but his early efforts caused little stir. However, in New York, which had experienced many revivals, he grew to be much loved. His tall stature, clear voice, and passionate delivery drew great crowds. He challenged people to commit themselves to Christ there and then. He was strong on the need for personal decision, and his Arminianism was in striking contrast to the general Calvinism of the day, and would have appalled Jonathan Edwards had he still been alive. Later on, Finney divided his time between teaching at Oberlin College and conducting revival meetings. His message was biblical enough, but he stressed the free will of human beings (as opposed to divine election) and was full of direct challenge. He made real changes in the contemporary understanding of evangelism. Whereas Whitefield and Edwards saw revivals as outpourings of God's blessings that humans can do nothing to create, Finney saw them as the proper application of proclamation and challenge. Another of Finney's achievements was to bring evangelism to the rapidly growing cities. He was the first to engage in mass evangelism. He abandoned the three-day pattern of the camp meetings because city dwellers could not afford the time to be away from their business for such a long period. Instead, he ran protracted revivals in the evenings only, and for a month or six weeks. He also pioneered various other approaches that we now take for granted: prayer meetings before he arrived for the revival, handbills and advertisements in local papers, door to door witness with an invitation to the meetings, the use of modern music and of trained laymen to counsel sinners sitting on "the anxious bench." Later evangelists, particularly Moody, tended to build on Finney's methods. There is much to learn from Finney. He had a strong sense of urgency in his preaching. He spent hours in prayer each day. He related his sermons to everyday life, which he was able to do effectively because he did a lot of visiting in the community. And as a former attorney, Finney preached for a verdict.

Dwight L. Moody

But it was Moody who took urban evangelism to new heights. Nobody in his rural township of Northfield would have imagined that Moody would become a world-famous evangelist. His father, a stonemason and small farmer, died, partly from the effects of drink, when Moody was only four and left his mother with the burden of raising nine children on a small farm. Finances were very tight. So as soon as he was eleven, Moody was taken out of school and put to work on the farm. He never received any further education, and he was never ordained. He is a classic demonstration of the apostle's claim that God chose "what is foolish in the world to shame the wise" (1 Corinthians 1:27). He was glad to escape from this bleak little farm at the age of seventeen, and he went to Boston and secured a job as a clerk in his uncle's shoe business. But in order to get the job, Moody had to promise to go to church regularly. He joined a Sunday school class at the Mount Vernon Congregational Church, and also the YMCA for recreational activities. Though he was deemed spiritually obtuse, he gradually began to absorb something of the Christian message. One day in 1855 his Sunday school teacher, Edward Kimball, went to talk to him about his salvation. He found Moody ready to respond, and then and there in the back room of the shoe store, he entrusted his life to Christ. He was still very unclear about it all. He applied for membership of the church but was turned down because, when asked what Christ had done for him, he replied, "I don't know. I think Christ has done a good deal for me. But I don't think of anything particular as I know of." Two kindly deacons were assigned to help him, and the following year he was accepted!

In 1856 Moody moved to Chicago and worked with his cousin Frank in a shoe store. He soon made a mark in business, which he loved. He prospered, and he used his money to purchase land. Indeed, he bought a small farm back in his home area of Northfield, where he would retire for much-needed rest and where, later on, he ran training conferences. Meanwhile his faith was developing, and two years later he started his own Sunday school for children from the roughest part of the city. It grew amazingly, and this prompted him in 1861 to give up business, albeit reluctantly, and devote himself full time to the YMCA, of which he became director and chief fundraiser. He soon became a popular speaker at YMCA conventions, and in 1864 he founded what is now known as the Moody Memorial Church. He did not fight in the Civil War as he was a conscientious objector, though he served for a while as a lay chaplain. But he soon devoted most of his time to itinerant evangelism.

In 1871 the Great Fire of Chicago destroyed the YMCA, his home and mission base, and for a while he was deeply depressed. But it led to a profound encounter with God, which he called his Pentecost: it changed his emphasis from Christian social work to evangelization. By 1873 the evidence began to show. Moody, and Ira Sankey, his song leader, visited Britain and conducted evangelistic meetings in England and Scotland. His message was much the same as before, but there was a new power in his ministry, the power of the Holy Spirit. His meetings created an enormous stir, and he returned to America as a celebrated evangelist. Between 1885 and 1888 Moody and Sankey preached and sang at crusades all over the United States. Observers estimated that the total attendance in New York alone was one and a half million, and that over the course of his life he must have been heard by one hundred million and led a million to the Lord.

Moody's Message

What was the message that stirred such numbers? The second part of the nineteenth century was a time of great industrial, intellectual, and social change. Could Moody's very simple message work among the urban masses? He rejected evolution and had no time for the popular higher criticism of the Bible. He was a fundamentalist: he spent much time studying the Bible, and if he saw a truth emphasized there, he would preach it. He was not attractive in himself. Though warm in temperament, he was overweight, unlettered, and uncouth, but he knew how to speak directly to men's hearts. He laid no claim to theological learning but was passionate about three central themes: the lost state of human beings, the atoning blood of Jesus, and the need for regeneration by the Holy Spirit. He did not pressure people for decision: he left that to the Holy Spirit. His job was to explain and apply the teaching of the Bible with Jesus as the central focus, for as he put it in *The Great Redemption*, "Christianity is not a dogma; it is not a creed; it is not a doctrine; it is not a feeling; it is not an impression; but it is a person." Accordingly, Moody's preaching was notable for its simplicity. He used words anyone could understand and never lost his touch with the underprivileged class from which he came, though, as he was something of a novelty, he drew many of the wealthy, the aristocratic, and the intelligent to his meetings. Often they came to mock and stayed to pray. He frequently used a visual aid that he called "the wordless book" when speaking to illiterate people. Apparently invented by Spurgeon, it worked with three colors: the bottom one black for the human condition, the middle one red for the atoning work of Christ, and the top one white for the justified sinner, counted as righteous through Christ. Moody added gold, to represent the heaven to which God was calling people. He knew Hudson Taylor, the pioneer missionary in China, and introduced him to the wordless book, thus facilitating cross-cultural mission. This was enhanced when the famous Cambridge Seven went to China after they had been brought to Christ by Moody in the Cambridge University mission of 1882. Moody never lost his love for the work in China.

His impact on Britain, after an unpropitious start, was enormous. Edinburgh was the key. He was invited there by a committee representing the Free Churches. They promised to prepare the ground if he accepted. Moody was aghast. How would his racy, anecdotal style and simple words go down in this capital city, full of learned but dusty theology? If he failed here, he would be laughed out of Britain. But his eight-week campaign there was remarkably fruitful. He was so different from anyone they had ever heard. Here is a sample of his preaching.

> Another young man told me last night that he was too great a sinner to be saved. Why, they are the very men Christ came after! "This Man receiveth sinners and eateth with them" [Luke 15:2]. The only charge they could bring against Christ down here was that He was receiving bad men. . . . All you have got to do is to prove that you are a sinner, and I will prove that you have got a Saviour. And the greater the sinner, the greater the need you have of a Saviour. . . . If your sins rise up before you like a dark mountain, bear in mind that the blood of Jesus Christ cleanses from all sin. There's no sin so big, or so black, or so corrupt and vile, but the blood of Christ can cover it. So I preach the old Gospel again, "The Son of Man has come to seek and to save that which is lost" [Luke 19:10]. A friend of mine from Manchester was in Chicago a few years ago . . .

And Moody was off on another of his vivid illustrative stories.

Bible stories, vivid illustrations, and a passionate challenge to follow Christ were the main elements on the Moody menu. But they were interspersed with new songs by Sankey, which shocked and eventually thrilled those accustomed to the dreary metrical psalms they were used to. It was Moody who first realized the power of music in his meetings. Sankey would begin by leading the congregation in singing at the start of the meeting. A choir would then produce special numbers. Before the sermon, Sankey would sing a solo and another at the end to accompany Moody's invitation to go into the inquiry room. Many of these songs are contained in a book they jointly published called *Sacred Songs and Solos*. It was an enormous success.

The inquiry room was another virtual innovation of Moody's. He eschewed emotionalism in his addresses, realizing how quickly emotions could evaporate. But he invited inquirers to go to a separate room where trained laypeople and pastors, whom he called "personal workers," could deal with individual cases. They must "be patient and thorough dealing with each case, no hurrying from one to another. Wait patiently, and ply them with God's word, and think, oh! think what it is to win a soul for Christ, and don't grudge the time spent on one person." The whole thing was so different from the dry debates on predestination to which churchgoers had been subjected, with the impression given that God was primarily a God of wrath. The mission set Edinburgh alight. Much the same impact was felt in Glasgow, where he spent six weeks, and London, where he spent five months. Thousands came to Christ, both church people who had simply been puzzled by the complicated sermons to which they had been subjected, and the completely unchurched "common man."

Perhaps his greatest triumph was the week-long mission in Cambridge, for both town and gown, which he and Sankey led in 1882. They were greeted initially with academic disdain by the dons and ribald mirth by the undergraduates. But a week later Moody preached to more than two thousand students, and the response was tremendous. Two hundred students stood to confess Christ that night, and many of them, like the Cambridge Seven mentioned above, went abroad to spread the gospel—including the chief mocker on the first night, Gerald Lander, who became in due course a missionary bishop in China!

Stories about Moody are legion, but more important is to consider why God used this man so greatly and what he particularly contributed to the work of evangelism.

Dr. R. A. Torrey, the first principal of the Moody Bible Institute (another of Moody's creations) and himself a distinguished evangelist who succeeded Moody, wrote a short book after his friend's death. He knew Moody very well, and he suggested that there were perhaps seven reasons why God used this man so signally. First, because he was totally surrendered to God. Second, he was a man of profound and believing prayer. Third, he was a deep and practical student of the Bible. Fourth, he was a man of great humility who hated drawing attention to himself: he wanted it all to go to his master. Fifth, he was entirely free of the love of money and was most generous with what he had. Sixth, he had a consuming passion for the salvation of the lost and sought every day to introduce someone to Christ. Seventh, he was a man who had been baptized with power from on high and was full of the Holy Spirit.

What did he particularly contribute as an evangelist? The list is a long one, and the effects remain today. First, he changed the "revival" led by a single preacher into a mission with the aim not so much of reviving sleepy Christians as winning new ones. Second, as a businessman, he applied business principles to evangelism. He generally succeeded in pulling together all the evangelical churches in a city to work together without any concern for denomination. A steering committee was put in place with subcommittees to handle finance, prayer, music and widespread publicity. Some criticized him for advertising

his services: it was undignified. "It is a good deal more undignified to preach to empty pews," was his reply. Ushers, choir
members, and "personal workers" were recruited and trained.
A large auditorium was rented, or a temporary "tabernacle"
constructed (sometimes this was portable!). Instead of long
theological sermons, Moody's sermons were short, punchy,
biblical, and well illustrated, culminating in a clear challenge
to repentance and faith. Moody developed the idea of the inquiry room, which Finney had inaugurated, and in later years
he started using decision cards. This was an important innovation. It not only helped inquirers to take a definite step, but
it enabled accurate records to be kept and names to be passed
on to local pastors for follow-up. Perhaps the combination of
music and preaching was his most significant innovation. John
Mark Terry explains in *Evangelism: A Concise History*: "Moody
used several different musicians in his career, but he worked
with Ira Sankey during the 1870s, his most active period of
evangelism. Sankey's winsome music attracted many to the
meetings." As Moody modestly put it, "The people come to
hear Sankey sing, and then I catch them in the gospel net."
Although he had so little formal education himself, he was
strongly persuaded of the importance of education in general—he founded two schools—but also in evangelism. His
training, his conferences at Northfield, his publications, and
his founding of the Bible College that became Moody Bible
Institute were all innovative and significant. Looking over his
ministry, it is clear that many of the methods he adopted or
inaugurated have continued in crusade evangelism to this day.
They certainly influenced Billy Graham.

Billy Graham

Billy Graham grew up on a dairy farm near Charlotte, North
Carolina. In 1934 this tall, handsome young man finally yielded
to the repeated invitations of a friend and went to a tent meet-

ing led by Mordecai Ham. This led him to Christ, and soon he was organizing Bible studies at his school. After school he enrolled first with Bob Jones University but transferred to the Florida Bible Institute in Tampa. While studying he made a considerable impact through evangelistic meetings for young people. During further studies at Wheaton College in 1943, he married Ruth Bell, and he offered to join the military as a chaplain. This did not materialize, but in the same year he was offered a local radio program called *Songs in the Night* and persuaded George Beverly Shea, a local radio executive, to produce the program and handle the music. They gained a considerable local following. But the next year Billy had a significant opportunity. He was asked to give the first address at the Chicagoland Youth for Christ (YFC) rally, and forty-two professed faith. Shortly afterwards, Graham became a full-time worker for Youth for Christ, and crisscrossed America speaking primarily at YFC gatherings, some of them large.

But he gained national celebrity in 1949 when he conducted his first crusade in Los Angeles, and in the next year he set up the Billy Graham Evangelistic Association. He always loved to work with a team, and the main players have continued loyal and grown old with him. In 1951 he was able to recruit Dawson Trotman, the founder of Navigators, to his team. Trotman was an expert in the follow-up of new believers, and this was an area in which the Graham organization had been weak. In 1953 Graham produced his most famous book, *Peace with God*, and he began to write a syndicated daily column for many newspapers, called "My Answer."

The big breakthrough outside America was in 1954 with the famous Harringay Crusade, which continued for no less than twelve weeks. It was organized by an interdenominational committee but opened in an atmosphere of great suspicion from the Church of England hierarchy and the press. However, it ended with Billy Graham, flanked by the lord mayor of London and the archbishop of Canterbury, preaching to a capacity crowd of more than 125,000 people in Wembley Stadium, the largest outdoor venue in the capital. The country was on the verge of a major turning to God. One has to wonder if that could have happened had Billy stayed longer and had local churches cashed in on the unparalleled interest in spiritual things.

People from all backgrounds came to faith, and the theological colleges were soon flooded with men who had surrendered to Christ at Harringay. Graham was the talk of society gatherings as well as the men in the pub who normally had nothing to do with religion. His approach followed that of Moody to a large extent: simple biblical preaching, concentrating on human need and God's offer of salvation, delivered with warmth and illustrated by many stories. Each address culminated in a firm but unemotional challenge to people who wanted to respond to Christ to "get up out of your seats and come to the front." Vast numbers did just that. God had anointed this man to be his special agent in calling England back to God. His sermons were not particularly memorable, and plenty of preachers did as well on their day, but the power of God was upon him and the response was massive. Those who came forward were counseled individually, their names and details taken, and these were passed on to pastors of local churches, irrespective of denomination. Not all of these continued in the Christian life, but this perhaps reflects more the failure of the follow-up in local churches rather than anything wrong with the evangelist's message.

Graham was now one of the most famous people in the world, and the world cried out for him to come and conduct crusades in their country. This he did, indefatigably, in all five continents, completing more than four hundred crusades. Unlike many evangelists, he refused to boost his own role but worked closely with his team: it was a shared enterprise, and they were all careful to give credit to God. He also ensured that each crusade was prepared in great detail—gaining support from different churches, publicity, finance, radio and television, follow-up material, and so forth, but above all prayer. In contrast to Moody, Graham prepared each address with great care and then gave himself to pray for the power of the Holy Spirit without which his words would be useless. He adapted brilliantly to the different nationalities and religious backgrounds that confronted him, and he made full use of testimony, music, film, radio, and print media. He was ecclesiastically colorblind, and he had a great gift for gaining support not only from evangelicals but from the Roman Catholic Church and the Orthodox as well. He also had an enviable skill in deflecting unjustified criticism and exhibiting Christian love and humility. He was a man it was very hard to hate! His integrity, courtesy, and sheer sincerity combined with his powerful biblical message to win hearts and minds for Christ wherever he went, be they Communist countries, India, Australia, New Zealand, or his native America. In every crusade he ran a School of Evangelism, training others to follow his steps. There has never been an evangelist like him since the apostolic age, and his life remained free from any hint of sexual or financial impropriety. He always ensured that his secretary slept in a different hotel from himself, and all the funds he raised went to charity or the Billy Graham Evangelistic Organization, which paid him and his team members a modest annual salary. His family bear testimony that he was always the same at home as he was in public. Their love for him is moving.

The other great and innovative landmark in his ministry was the Lausanne Congress in 1974. This was a truly international gathering of some four thousand ministers and laypeople with a passion for evangelism. It was not dominated by Americans and English but had larger representation from countries in the two-thirds world where evangelism was proving far more effective than in the West. This was a remarkable transdenominational consideration of and stimulus to evangelism by a worldwide gathering, and it spawned massively increased outreach in many parts of the world. It also healed a yawning breach that had opened up since the 1910 Edinburgh Conference for world evangelism, between the evangelicals with their stress on personal salvation and the more liberal churchmen who concentrated increasingly on social concern. The social dimension of evangelism was stressed as strongly as the evangelistic at Lausanne, and this balanced vision rescued evangelical Christianity from other-worldly pietism. The Lausanne Covenant was passed almost unanimously after various revisions, and it became a major missiological statement, commanding widespread discussion, in the decades that followed. Another wise result of Lausanne was the refusal to set up a world evangelical structure to rival the more liberal World Council of Churches, but rather the decision to authorize a low-powered committee to continue the aims of Lausanne. This continues to this day and is proving immensely fruitful and innovative.

Billy refused to give up as bereavement struck and age began to grip him. His influence seemed only to increase worldwide as a wise, gracious, and loving counselor, who had close relationships with successive American presidents and international leaders. He proved to be a gifted peacemaker in the painfully divided societies of South Africa and Ireland. I recall his great evangelistic rally in Durban in 1973 at the height of apartheid, when both the government and the Dutch Reformed Church were deeply suspicious of his presence in the country. The King's Park rugby stadium was absolutely packed, and Billy spoke with charm and simplicity. After his appeal the place went wild and some four thousand surged forward like a mighty tide. The counselors could not cope, having expected about fifteen hundred based on the statistical average. I saw packets of follow-up material thrown at random into the enormous crowd! This crusade had an immediate impact on the whole country, but unfortunately those who came forward to profess faith did not all get the help they needed. It was the first time South Africans of every social level and color had seen the civilizing and unifying power of a really large interracial Christian gathering, and they loved it. I noticed that the armed guards at the gates were in tears, to see blacks, whites, and Indians seated so amicably together, and thousands kneeling to pour out their hearts at the foot of the cross. I was sitting on the turf with black people all round me, and I shall never forget their wonder and joy. It was a foretaste of the political and social integration that would inevitably come later.

Billy Graham had determined to preach the gospel until the very end of his life, and so he did, by radio and television even when he was too frail to stand in a pulpit. At his funeral, attended by all the living American presidents apart from Obama, the gospel he had given his life to was proclaimed afresh and several thousand professions of faith were recorded.

Billy was not just a preacher. He and his organization produced almost a hundred films, the most famous of which was *The Hiding Place*. Initially they used landlines to take the message to different venues, and then television. Equally, their use of radio was superb. By 1958 the *Hour of Decision* program was heard by about twenty million people a week. His books sold widely—*Peace with God* sold over a million copies. His organization started *Decision* magazine, which quickly exceeded the circulation of all other religious magazines: it had a circulation of two million. He helped his son Franklin launch the worldwide Samaritan's Purse to meet the physical needs of the poorest in the world and respond to natural disasters. He shared pulpits with Martin Luther King to encourage the collapse of apartheid. He used his influence with highly placed politicians to stress that a country had to be ethical to be great. Here at last was an evangelist with an all-round ministry.

It is no exaggeration to say that Billy Graham became evangelist to the world. He addressed more people than any other preacher has ever done. He loved working with young people and on nine occasions spoke at the great international student Urbana Congress, urging his hearers to live their whole lives for God: he often quoted the six words of the famous missionary Borden of Yale, "No reserve, no retreat, no regrets." He even made mass evangelism respectable. But questions remain as to its long-term fruitfulness. It has been estimated that some 60 percent of those who attended the crusades of Moody and Graham were already church members. Most of those who went forward at Billy's appeal were not to be seen later on in churches. For example, in Graham's second crusade in the United Kingdom, in the Kelvin Hall in Glasgow, 52,253 decisions were registered. But only 3,802 people joined a local church as a result. He himself said, "I have come to the conclusion that the most important phase is the follow-up." It is also the hardest, as most evangelists find.

Was there a weakness in the message preached? Was the cost of discipleship insufficiently stressed? Was there a sense of peer pressure or curiosity that led so many people to go forward who had made no lasting commitment to Christ? Did much of the fault lie with inadequately trained counselors or the failure of the local churches to care pastorally for the names given them? Did concentration on big, exciting crusades tend to encourage churches to pay too much attention to the special event, to the detriment of year-long local evangelism? The jury is out on these questions. But although mass evangelism needs to be balanced by continuous local outreach, and careful follow-up, the impact of a Moody and a Graham can hardly be exaggerated. They brought Christ before literally millions, many of whom would never have heard of him. Moody's preaching slashed the crime rate, and Graham's led to racial integration, a new desire to cooperate across denominational boundaries, and an awareness that evangelism is genuinely possible in highly secularized countries. Both demonstrated that God is on the move and available to all who call on him. This itself has proved an immense encouragement to Christians across the world.

For Reflection

1. What are the most important innovations in evangelism introduced by Moody and Graham? How are they relevant today?
2. Reflect on the strengths and weaknesses of mass evangelism and revivalism.
3. To what extent was the fruitfulness of Graham's ministry due to meticulous preparation and working as a team?
4. How is it that an unlettered, untrained preacher like D. L. Moody, who was never ordained and never belonged to a denomination, made such an impact?
5. How essential is integrity and sincerity, compared with theological acumen and careful preparation, for effective mission?
6. Finney, Moody, and Graham were all very ordinary men, of no great education, all significantly humble—how significant was this for their success?
7. All three evangelists were keen to attribute glory to God for the work, not to claim it for themselves. Is this a common characteristic today?

12

My Sixty Years in Evangelism

It is fascinating to look back over the years and to reflect on how often Christians have needed to dress the unchanging gospel in new clothes! I want in this chapter to reflect on my own experience of evangelism, lessons I have learned, and changes I have seen. It was in the 1950s that I first led a friend to Christ. I began to engage in public evangelism shortly after that. Indeed, I recall the first time I was invited to preach evangelistically at Oxford University. I was terrified and wondered if I dared ask inquirers to stay behind. I did, and several people came to Christ, which was an enormous encouragement to me. In those days the majority of people in this country had absorbed something of a Christian background. There were no other faiths in the UK marketplace at the time, only the usual British apathy. So the job of the evangelist was to clarify and enforce what people vaguely agreed with, and then to challenge them to respond. We did not do a lot of apologetics or even testimony. Preaching was an accepted part of most people's lives, and if it was vibrant they tended to listen, and many responded.

A Golden Era

The 1950s saw the first Billy Graham missions in the United Kingdom. He had started these in 1949 in the United States, and I remember a keen Christian soldier, General Wilson Haffenden, telling me in 1952 when he came to the Oxford University Christian Union, of which I happened to be president, that he and some friends were going to take the risk of inviting the young evangelist to England. Well, the result is history. It had an enormous impact on the country despite initial ecclesiastical opposition. Harringay Arena was packed night after night, and countless people, including Cliff Richard, professed faith. The follow-up, given over as it was to the churches, was very patchy, but there is general agreement that England was nearer to a revival in 1954 than at any time since the 1860s. It did not quite happen. But still the impact was enormous. I was starting out as a theological college tutor in the late 1950s, and the college was packed with students who had come to faith through Billy Graham. This was a golden era. John Stott, rector of All Souls Langham Place, was Billy's main assistant at the London Crusade, and they were close friends. Stott's work at All Souls was strategic and very important. It was he who first devised the idea of guest services, he who first trained the congregation in considerable depth to become personal workers, and he who led the way in effective evangelistic preaching in universities. It was a privilege to know him quite well and learn from him: he even preached at our wedding. He remained throughout his long life one of the best evangelists I have ever heard, and he used nothing apart from Scripture, his personal graciousness, and his voice. There were many in those days who took their cue from Graham and Stott. It became typical in many an evangelical church to have several evangelistic guest services in the year, each followed by an after meeting rehearsing the way of salvation. Though crusades were not attempted apart from Luis Palau, large-scale evangelistic meetings definitely were. This was accompanied by a great deal of Christian social work. It was certainly not mere preaching.

But the mood in England began to change. There was more skepticism in the sixties, accompanied by sexual liberation based on the pill. It was only then that the country really began to recover after the war, and pop music became innovative and widely influential. Some of it was love song, some confident about the future, but much of it nihilistic and despondent. Some of us realized that if we were going to continue to win people for Christ, we needed to make two adjustments to our message.

Addressing the Culture Through Apologetic and Books

One was the increasing need for good apologetic as society became more and more secularized, and the other was the importance of keeping in tune with the feelings and moods of the day, best expressed by the artists and song writers. It was then that I started writing—quite by accident. I was constantly being asked to do so, and constantly refused. And then at one conference Francis Schaeffer and I were both speaking. I urged him to write: he said he was no good at it. So, because he was having such an influence among British evangelicals through his talks and tapes, I suggested that I should get someone to ghost him. And that is how his first book emerged! After that he simply took off and became the first effective modern apologist, really wrestling with the issues of the secular world. I was very struck by his method: it was dialectical, like Socrates, and he listened carefully to the worldview that was being expressed and he then remorselessly drove its proponent back into self-contradiction and showed him that he could not live with it. It was at that point that people's innate humanity trumped their mistaken ideology. I learned from him to drive people back to the logic of their presuppositions.

Meanwhile, I had reluctantly started writing myself: the first book, *Choose Freedom*, was simply a series of addresses I had given in my first overseas mission to the University of

Cape Town with Dick Lucas. It was not a very good book, but it sold extensively and had to be reprinted time after time. Why? Well, first, it had a lovely cover of a blue sky with a seagull, whereas most Christian books of the day were very dreary in presentation. And second, the content was so different from other Christian books. In those days people wrote in a somewhat elevated style, including the main evangelistic book of the day, John Stott's *Basic Christianity*, but my material was idiomatic, just as I spoke. It had an immediate appeal and in fact changed the way evangelicals addressed writing. I was asked to do another book, and used a current TV title, *Man Alive*, to explore whether the resurrection happened and what difference it made. That went into over thirty languages and impacted people in many parts of the world. I gather that it led many to become missionaries or pastors. It was a mix of academic integrity and copious illustrations, and it caught the mood of the day. When it came out in a new guise fifteen years later, it made no significant impact at all. As in sport, it is all a question of getting the timing right, and you never know if you have done it until after publication, when it soars or bombs! The next book, *Runaway World*, grappled with the apologetic issues of the day, such as communism and psychology, in a way nothing else at the time did, and I was warned by the publishers it was a bit heavy and might not sell like *Man Alive*. This proved not to be the case. The impact was even greater, and it was one of only two religious books since the war reviewed by the *Daily Mirror*. I think the reviewer read only the first chapter dealing with the historical evidence for Jesus. He was amazed that there was so much—hence the review appearing in the *Mirror*, most of whose readers would have shared the reviewer's assumption that there was not much evidence for Jesus. At this time, coffee house evangelism was the rage, and it led George Carey, who later became archbishop of Canterbury, to Christ. It has currently fallen into disuse but may well revive: it works particularly well in Serbia at present.

My Sixty Years in Evangelism

Charismatic Evangelism

It was apparent that the culture was moving further away from Christianity, and that the church was failing to cope with it. So, as we moved into the seventies, David Watson and I were able to give a new twist to evangelistic outreach. We both led influential churches, he in York and myself in Oxford, and it was through David that I, and then our church St. Aldate's, added a charismatic dimension to our biblical Christianity. The received wisdom of the day, at least in student evangelistic circles, was to avoid any song or hymn in case people were required to sing it without believing it. But David and I came to see that worship is one of the prime ways in which God reaches into the soul, and that the evangelistic enterprise should embody creativity as well as revelation. So our services became very different, in the church and in the university and the parish missions we were conducting. We both made use of illustrations from popular songs and literature. We both used drama imaginatively, not simply as a precursor to the talk but as part of it to make a point succinctly and give a change of voice and recall folk to full attention. So we encouraged a drama group to form and used them often, either employing the brilliant Riding Lights sketches or producing their own. Both churches already had music groups, using worship songs as well as hymns, and now we both developed dance groups, a development of Israeli circle dancing. We used this outside the church in the street and it brought people in. We used it in worship, too. There is an important difference between drama and dance. Drama is designed to illuminate the mind, whereas dance is designed to lift the soul in worship. Both are invaluable assets to proclamation. We also made extensive use of carefully monitored testimony, which took the truth that was being taught and showed that it was real in a person's life. So the testimony could come at any stage in the evangelistic proceedings. We discovered that it was even more effective if we interviewed the person concerned, particularly on what

143

life was like before conversion, how it happened, and the difference it made.

David died at the height of his powers in 1984, aged fifty, when he was becoming recognized as the most significant clergyman in the country, with major celebratory missions in cathedrals up and down the land, and heavily in demand overseas. David produced three widely selling books that were his university evangelistic addresses, and we both wrote extensively on doctrinal matters of concern to the Christian public, contributing to the *I Believe* series, which appeared simultaneously in the United Kingdom and the United States. Many of the volumes were translated into other languages. Recently I met a man who had read my *Evangelism in the Early Church* in Korean and was grateful for it! Looking back, I can see it was in a sense the end of an era. During the previous decade the charismatic movement had swept the country. Tongues, prophecies, healings, and deliverance ministry were parts of our regular ministry and sometimes emerged in our evangelism. People would occasionally collapse on the floor, or burst into tears, or suddenly receive the gift of tongues when nobody had even mentioned it. But historically evangelism, in times when the Spirit has been particularly active, has often been like this—untidy but full of life.

One Church's Outreach

From St. Aldate's we would do evangelism in a variety of ways. We ran well publicized evangelistic services that deeply affected both town and gown, preached and used drama and mime in the main streets of Oxford. Mime was particularly valuable among the vast overseas crowds, many of whom had no English, that jostled its streets in the summer. We did open-air proclamation on the crowded riverbanks during the rowing races. I would go into the college bars at the invitation of Christian students, debate the faith, and then invite those who were obviously moved to come and have lunch with me, one on one. This led to many conversions. We had public debates with well-known secularists, or we would defend the faith in the Debating Union. These drew big audiences, and they, too, led to conversions. Each year we took a massive mission, with a team of one hundred or more, to some part of the country when careful preparations had been made. At times during these big missions, we stopped traffic in the street with circle dancing. At times people lined the pavements trying to get into the meetings. We would often run open-air meetings, which were great fun. Not the "turn or burn" sort but something intriguing and attractive. We would make use of a juggler or some strong man who could break a plank across his knee, and this would draw a crowd. The compere would then start to speak but without notes and with great humor and welcome. He had to be good to hold the crowd. There would be a succession of short, sharp testimonies covering different aspects of the Christian life, repartee from the crowd, and a challenge to respond at the end. These open airs served mainly to involve members of the congregation and get them to fly the flag in public, but quite often we saw definite conversions from these open airs. Sometimes considerable crowds gathered to listen and watch, and our team would move in among them, engaging in personal evangelism.

Another feature of the work was what we called Agnostics Anonymous. This was a group of unbelievers gathered in our house to examine the Christian faith. Almost all of them were prompted to come by some Christian friend, and consequently they were all covered in prayer. We fed them and then encouraged them to say what they did not believe, while I said what I did believe and why, majoring on the person of Christ and the evidence for his resurrection. These were very effective interactive groups, and people gradually dropped off into "Beginners' Groups" as they came to Christ. Our hope was to have nobody left in the agnostic group by the end of the final, sixth session! There were lots of other initiatives in those heady days. We were often invited to preach in college chapels, and sometimes this would lead to conversions or the revival of dormant Christians.

Triumphant Secularism

Thereafter there seemed to be a dip in effective and innovative evangelism, but in the early 90s I was working in Canada and reintroducing evangelism in universities there after it had fallen into disuse. However, my impression is that there was less confident evangelism taking place in England during that decade, as secularism hardened and political correctness emerged (only to flourish much later after the equality legislation). I had sometimes been doing *Thought for the Day* on the BBC before I left, and I was able to be very direct. By the time I returned I found a very different climate and even the name "Jesus" was rarely heard on *Thought for the Day*. Secularism had triumphed in the 90s, and the Christians seem to have been driven onto the back foot. An attempt was made to remedy the situation by laying increasing weight on Christian apologetics, but apologetics without evangelism is a broken reed. It should be the handmaid to evangelism, the steppingstone to faith. But instead it became, I think, much more remote from the thought world of the average person, with theorists discussing the merits of different types of apologetics, and often starting so far back with philosophical issues that they did not get to Jesus at all. No wonder there was little fruit.

But the twenty-first century has seen a modest revival of confident preaching. The number of lively, active churches has significantly increased across the country, despite vast areas of wasteland, and church planting, led by Holy Trinity Brompton, has become a growth industry. It has been a challenge because the modernism that argued about other faiths and miracles has given way to a postmodernism that has different concerns. In the face of skepticism about absolutes in morals and truth, and an excessive subjectivism, a different approach has been required. The British population thinks Christianity has failed, just as the humanism that succeeded it has failed, leaving us with a selfish desire to go for "what seems good for me." People are mainly unwilling to engage with serious issues such as why there is anything rather than nothing, where we came from, and where we are heading. This will prove disastrous for society in the long run, and it makes it very hard for the evangelist.

Essentials If We Are to Be Heard

This is not the place for an extended examination of the way ahead, nor am I, at the age of eighty-eight, the person to give it. But here are some reflections that may be important.

Actions are more important than words. People are fed up with politicians and preachers. They will only start to inquire when they see what love in action looks like. Feeding the hungry, caring for orphans and widows, looking after the lonely, forming affordable housing associations—such things are not evangelism in themselves but are a necessary part of commending the gospel, as Jesus demonstrated so clearly. Love is the greatest thing in the world: it is the echo of the God we worship. People will not return to the great Lover until they see practical love in the lives of his followers. In the university world, cold water offered by Christian students to drunk partygoers at two a.m. is a wonderful start, as is the free food and drink offered in university missions, and the extensive social outreach of the churches. It raises the question, Why do these people do it? Lifestyle remains critical. If people in this broken society see some of their friends living by different standards, with purity, helpfulness, self-sacrifice, generosity, and concern for justice prominent in their lives, this is extremely attractive and it bears fruit.

A second challenge to modern evangelists is to get well informed about the tenets of Islam, together with the homosexual and transgender issues. Not that this will of itself make conversions. But if we know what we are talking about, we will get a hearing and have a chance gently to point to a better way.

Third, I think we need to move toward a different kind of apologetics. Ours has been directed, particularly in universities, toward the mind. In a recent mission that Bruce Gillingham and I led in Lancaster University, we went for the issues of the heart—loneliness, identity, love, and values that touch people deeply. We did not duck the academic issues, but we offered a free tea each day for people to come and engage with them, bringing any question they wished to raise. This is, of course, very challenging for the evangelist and apologist, but immensely satisfying for the inquirers, and it led at Lancaster to a much higher proportion of conversions.

Evangelists need to be careful not to underestimate the importance of worship. You only have to watch the World Cup to see worship that is far more extravagant than the wildest charismatics. People need something bigger than themselves to get excited about, and quality worship meets that need and draws people in.

We must have the courage of our convictions and not be afraid to express them, graciously but firmly, in the face of today's excessive political correctness. This quality seems to have been compromised by church leaders, but where it marks the Christian witness you generally find church growth. This courage needs to be matched by passion, which has a drawing power all of its own. It is like a flame, lit at

Calvary, and that flame is bright and attractive. But much of the modern church, at any rate in Britain, lacks passion.

It is unlikely that we will see massive advance until church members are deeply convinced of the truth of the gospel and utterly unafraid to commend it in all its winsome power to others. This needs to be done with creativity. We live too much in our church buildings. Our services are too predictable, too dull. We care more for what we have always done than for what new initiatives the Lord is calling us to take. So it is wise to incorporate in our public presentations drama and dance, poetry and story, drama and testimony, film clips and other means of furthering the cause we love.

Evangelists tend to think in terms of one-off presentations or perhaps a short mission. They must not forget that church planting has proved to be the most effective way of spreading the gospel worldwide in recent decades. A colleague of mine whose father was a publican used to say, "If you want to sell more beer you must open more pubs." It is sad to see so much money going into bricks and mortar in the Christian movement rather than into imaginative and cheap alternatives, such as hiring schools or pub rooms for worship and outreach, while having the church office set up cheaply in a rented shop front.

Effective evangelism in the digital age must make use of the web. The worldwide use of the web has broken through the need for literacy, and it makes immediate communication possible everywhere. I doubt if we have woken up yet to its evangelistic significance. Here is just one example. A student friend of mine at a theological college was a driver in the army before he started training for ordination. He worked for an atheist colonel who was well informed, since he had read theology at university. They had frequent debates despite the difference in rank. The colonel chose him for many journeys simply so that they could talk. They put their discussions up on the internet and soon there were hordes of people drawn into the discussion. It was like a honey pot.

In the end, evangelism is not rocket science. It comes down to one person who knows Christ relating to one person who does not. I remember Billy Graham at a breakfast for theological students at Cambridge. A professor questioned his use of mass evangelism. Billy's reply has stuck with me. "Mass evangelism is not the only way, or even the best way of spreading the gospel. One-to-one conversation is. But God has given me this way, and I want to use it responsibly for him." A friend of mine, Norman Warren, has majored on personal evangelism and trained hundreds of people in it using a very simple booklet, *Journey into Life*. He wrote it in 1963 and received several rejection slips before it was accepted. It has now sold over forty million, continues to be published at about a hundred thousand a year. He has trained hundreds of ordinary Christians to sit with a friend and go through that booklet, culminating in a commitment to Christ. That is just one example of the principle we have seen throughout this book, that God uses humble, ordinary people to spread his gospel. Jesus in the Gospels is often shown as concentrating on a single person. The way for the church to follow is precisely the same.

Through all the changes and challenges, God has remained faithful and the gospel has continued to grow across the world. It is sometimes discouraging in Europe, the hardest continent at present. But recall the state of British society at the start of the eighteenth century, sunk in poverty, immorality, and drunkenness. Within a generation, under the preaching of the Wesleys and Whitefield, the whole flavor of the country was transformed for the next hundred years. Or think of China, with Christians reduced to about a million when the missionaries were kicked out in 1950, now with more than one hundred million believers and growing, despite the attentions of the Communist government. What God has done, he can do again. Jesus really is Lord.

For Reflection

1. What changes have I noticed during my life both in the culture and in effective evangelism?
2. Why has Europe, once predominately Christian, moved so far away?
3. How would Jesus react to current issues such as sex, race, equality, and the sanctity of life?
4. Whom among the evangelists mentioned in this book do I most admire, and whom do I find most difficult. Why?
5. Has this book encouraged you to see what a magnificent task evangelism is? If so, what are you going to do about it?

Afterword

by Michael Ots

Michael said that he was not in a position, at the age of eighty-eight, to speak on the future of evangelism. I am less than half his age; yet I am not sure that I am in a position to predict the future either. (On missions we were often referred to as "the old Michael and the young Michael"—though his relentless energy and enthusiasm often left me wondering who the "young" one actually was!)

If the Covid-19 pandemic taught us anything, perhaps it is that we don't know what is coming! I remember being at a large Christian gathering at the start of 2020. At the conference confident predictions were made by some that we were on the verge of revival. In reality, we were on the verge of a pandemic, and, despite the unique evangelistic opportunities it afforded, it did not usher in a revival. God was still at work through it—but not in a way that anyone had expected.

Perhaps it is more prudent to identify current observable trends, and then consider how we might respond to them— while retaining a humility that accepts things may actually go in a very different direction to the one we might expect.

AFTERWORD

The Opportunities of the Internet

Michael spoke about the need to use the internet in evangelism. In many ways, the pandemic forced us all to do that. Perhaps it was a small mercy that Michael didn't live to see this season. He regularly forgot to turn on his older model of mobile phone, and I'm not sure how much he would have enjoyed the technological challenges. However, I don't doubt he would have made use of any opportunities. I remember him telling me, shortly before his death, that he was considering getting a smartphone.

The pandemic revealed some of the opportunities of "online evangelism." The Alpha Course reported far more people joining online courses than they had ever had in person. People could engage from the privacy (and "safety") of their own homes, and at a time that was convenient to them.

Google and YouTube are the world's two largest search engines. People turn to both, not simply to find out simple factual information or entertainment, but as a means to find answers to more personal and searching questions such as "How do I forgive?," "Who am I?," "Why do we have to die?" This provides a great opportunity for Christians to provide short and engaging answers to the questions people are asking. Many people are now far more likely to watch a video online than they are to go to a church service or evangelistic event in a building. I have met a number of people who came to faith in Christ through watching videos online—and only later made connection with Christians in person.

The Challenges of the Internet

While the internet provides unprecedented opportunities, it also presents us with challenges and has some serious limitations.

Many Christians, myself included, were slow to adapt our communication style for an online audience. Many preached sermons to the camera as if they were in church. We had to work hard at being more engaging and creating much shorter, pithier content—which answered the real questions that people are asking.

The realm of the internet can be a hard place to change people's minds. People are much more likely to watch or read things that confirm their existing beliefs than things that challenge them. Social media algorithms can encourage us into an echo chamber of our own making, where we are insulated from opposing ideas and beliefs.

Perhaps the biggest drawback of online evangelism is that it is arguably much more difficult to create community and to offer hospitality—yet these are two key factors often involved in drawing people to faith. So, while online evangelism has its place, I would argue that it will not and should not replace the need for in-person communication of the gospel. It seems the pandemic may wonderfully have taught us afresh not only the importance of Jesus's incarnation but the human need for real in-person connection.

Increasing Secular Hostility—Yet Increasing Openness to the Gospel

Secularization is a trend that Michael himself observed through his six decades in evangelism—a trend that has continued. While it presents challenges (many people have little to no understanding of the gospel), it also may mean that people are now more open to the gospel than they have been for many years.

When I started speaking at university mission weeks twenty years ago, a common point of connection was to take people's objections to the Christian faith as a starting point, with talk titles that would spark curiosity to come along: "Why would God allow suffering?" or "How can there be only one way to God?," etc. Consequently, my first book, *What Kind of God?*, dealt with a number of these moral objections that had been voiced by the so-called New Atheists.

It seemed that many atheists were rejecting the (often nominal) religion of their parents. This is not the case today. Most young people I find today have had no exposure to any form of Christianity and aren't even aware of such objections. I was recently on a university mission in Croatia, and the students were doing a survey on the campus, asking, "Does the existence of suffering disprove the existence of God?" To our surprise, almost everyone said no. When asked why, people seemed confused as to why suffering would have anything to do with God!

This doesn't mean that people are not asking questions. It's just that they don't necessarily see how God is connected to the things that they care deeply about. Instead of asking "Why does God allow suffering?," they might be asking, "Is there any purpose to my suffering?"; instead of "How can there be one way to God?," the question might now be, "How can we have peace in a divided world?" We need to work hard to show the relevance of the Christian faith to every area of life. While people may be apathetic about traditional religion, they are not apathetic about *everything*—quite the opposite! Young people are now more likely to be socially concerned and ethically conservative than their parents. Street protests in recent years have indeed revealed a strength of passion for racial and gender equality, as well as environmental concern. What many don't realize, though, is that the gospel is the ultimate basis for such things.

I see three trends in western culture that present us with great opportunities to show the beauty and relevance of the gospel.

Three Trends That Provide Opportunities

The Need for Community

In a recent talk, Nick Spencer (of THEOS Think Tank) commented that the growth of the welfare state has caused many people to think that the church is now redundant. What was once a vital source of provision in areas such as education and health care is now seen as "unnecessary." However, while there have been huge advances in the standard of living in the last fifty years, this doesn't mean that people's experience of life is now any better. A quarter of the people in the United Kingdom today take antidepressants. One of the reasons for this may well be people's increasing isolation and loneliness.

Europe is a continent with increasingly lonely inhabitants. While it was traditionally thought that the elderly were the most lonely, studies show that young people are now twice as likely to experience loneliness as older Europeans.

This can be an amazing opportunity for the church to be a people/place where people experience real community and loving welcome. Rather than waiting for people to come to faith before inviting them into the community of the church, it is often the case that people have a need to belong somewhere before they come to believe. This need to belong doesn't just mean having one's own needs met; it can actually mean being given the opportunity to meet the needs of others.

The Need for Forgiveness

Many social commentators have noted how we have become an increasingly judgmental culture. The motives behind what has been dubbed "cancel culture" may be good ones—a right anger at injustices like racism and inequality—but the consequence of this sort of culture can also be a lack of anyone ever imparting or finding forgiveness. Mistakes committed in our teenage years can come back to haunt us in later life.

In such a culture, the offer of Jesus's forgiveness may actually be particularly appealing! God doesn't tolerate our sin; the demands of justice must be met. *But*—in Christ—God was able to both satisfy the need for justice and offer us his free forgiveness. If the church can both preach and model forgiveness, then this may be especially attractive to those looking on. (The real and present danger, however, is that we become like the culture, and attack each other.)

The Need for Hope

The Covid-19 pandemic, the ongoing environmental crisis, the outbreak of war in Europe and the associated economic crises have made people increasingly fearful about the future. After decades of relative security, the threat of global conflict now seems alarmingly real. This has been a challenge to the commonly held post-Enlightenment view that everything is inevitably going to get better.

In such a climate, Christian hope, based on the foundation of the resurrection of Christ, can shine especially brightly! If this is both preached and modeled in the everyday lives of believers, the gospel may be especially compelling in our current culture.

Society may think that the church is irrelevant to life, but in a judgmental world, full of much fear and loneliness, it is the gospel of God that offers welcome, forgiveness, and hope.

Committing Ourselves to the Future

It is now more than three years since Michael died, yet I think of him often and miss him deeply. Of course, I miss our friendship, which grew through the many missions we did together, and the fun that we had. However, what I miss the most is his enthusiasm for Jesus, and for sharing him, that was such an obvious inspiration to many. I often felt like a battery being recharged with evangelistic zeal when I spent time with Michael!

After Michael's funeral service, there was an open time of sharing during which many friends told stories that illustrated how Michael had been such an inspirational example to them. At the end of the afternoon, his wife, Rosemary, shared a few final words. She commented that after everything that had been shared, she wanted to resolve to commit herself afresh to the work of evangelism.

I hope reading this book has had a similar impact on you. Whatever the future holds, let us commit ourselves fully to the work of sharing the best news in the world. Let us keep "fresh" to the winds of culture, in serving God and others in the inimitable style of Michael Green; for we can know, as he did, that "our labor in the Lord is not in vain."

Index

Edwards, John, 88, 124
election, doctrine of: Calvin,
73–74; Finney, 124; Simeon,
104
English eighteenth- and
nineteenth-century evangelical initiatives, 96–110; the
Clapham Sect, 99–103, 105,
106; imaginative evangelistic
clergy (the "enthusiasts"),
96–99; Shaftesbury and Victorian age reforms, 106–9,
111; Simeon and church
leadership, 98, 103–6;
Wilberforce and antislavery
campaigns, 99–103
English Evangelical Revival
(eighteenth century), 84–95,
106; the class meeting, 91–
92; holy living and lifestyles,
93–95; hymns of Charles
Wesley, 91, 92–93; "new
birth," 86, 87, 89, 94; Wesley,
85–95; Whitefield, 85–95, 97,
124. *See also* English eigh-
teenth- and nineteenth-century evangelical initiatives
English Reformation, 76–82;
Book of Homilies, 80; martyrs and evangelists, 79–82;
Prayer Books of 1549 and
1552, 78, 80–81; Tyndale's
English Bible, 77
environmental crisis, 156, 158
Ephesus, 12, 18, 21, 23–24, 36

Epictetus, 15
Epistle to Diognetus, The, 25–27
Erasmus of Rotterdam, 68, 77
Eusebius, 35, 36
Evangelicals (Church of En-
gland), 92, 96–99
Evangelism: A Concise History
(Terry), 131
Evangelism in the Early Church
(Green), vii, viii, xiii, 144
Evangelism Now and Then
(Green), xiii
*Evangelism through the Local
Church* (Green), vii–viii, xiii
exorcism, 4, 8, 35–37

Factories Acts, 108
Fellowship of Evangelists in
the Universities of Europe
(FEUER), x
Finney, Charles, 124–25, 131
Finney, John, 53
first Christians. *See* early
Christian evangelists
Flavius Clemens, 41
Fletcher of Madeley, 98–99
Florida Bible Institute, 132
forgiveness, the need for,
157–58
Foxe's *Book of Martyrs*, 81
Francis of Assisi, 61
Francke, Hermann, x
Frederick of Saxony, 70
Free Churches, 128
French Revolution, 99, 105
Fuller Seminary, x